D0848514

My History Is America's History

15 Things You Can Do
To Save
America's Stories

A millennium project of

THE NATIONAL ENDOWMENT FOR THE HUMANITIES

in partnership with

THE WHITE HOUSE MILLENNIUM COUNCIL

*We wish to thank the families who have
been so generous in contributing
their personal stories and
memorabilia to this endeavor.*

Guidebook to "My History Is America's History"
published by The National Endowment for the Humanities
Washington, D.C. 1999
ISBN: 0-942310-00-4 (pbk.)

   My History Is America's History
   1. American history. 2. American family history.
3. Family history.

Library of Congress Catalog Card Number: 99-76568

Our History Is America's History

Follow your family's history and you will discover America's history. That is the theme of **My History Is America's History,** an exciting new project created by the National Endowment for the Humanities to mark the new millennium. **My History** offers all of us a way to explore family history as we discover how our own family stories connect to the history of our nation. By gathering together our family stories, **My History** will weave a powerful tapestry of America that illustrates our nation's history and culture.

William R. Ferris

Many Americans are historians without being aware of it. Each of us has stories we pass, like family heirlooms, from generation to generation. These stories define us and connect us to distant places and significant events. You can start your own family history with a single old photo, letter, or a family tale that you save as a legacy for generations to come.

Our guidebook provides 15 ways that you can preserve family memories and treasures through activities that make history an exciting adventure for your entire family, complete with many examples of how other families have discovered and saved their own stories.

Our website is a virtual "front porch" for every American. Once you enter www.myhistory.org, you can explore other tales that will help you understand your own stories and those of your ancestors. Once you post your family stories and photographs in the online collection, you can discover more about your ancestors as you create your family tree and see how each branch connects with the nation's history.

We developed **My History Is America's History** with the generous support of many partners. Major contributors include the White House Millennium Council, the President's Committee on the Arts and the Humanities, Genealogy.com, PSINet Inc., and the National Association of Broadcasters.

I invite you to pull up a rocking chair on our NEH virtual front porch and rediscover America through **My History Is America's History**. As you preserve your own family history, you help build a national treasure that will enrich future generations.

William Ferris

William R. Ferris
Chairman
National Endowment for the Humanities

I am delighted to be a part of **My History Is America's History**—a project of the National Endowment for the Humanities and an official project of the White House Millennium Council. The approach of the new millennium is a unique moment in our history. It is a time to *honor the past and imagine the future.* One of the best ways for all of us to do this is to compile our own family histories.

Hillary Rodham Clinton

My History can help us appreciate who we are, where we come from, and what we want from the future both individually and as a nation. This project will help us explore, preserve, and share our family histories and treasures.

We can start by sharing and recording the family stories and memories that are passed down from generation to generation. This is a wonderful and important way to bring families together and to strengthen the bonds between children and their parents, grandparents, and other family members.

I recall how I loved to listen to my father recount incidents that occurred in his life when he was a young man. Learning about the lives of my parents and grandparents and other relatives told me so much not only about them, but about myself as well. Our families, the times in which they lived, and the events that shaped their lives are an important backdrop for our lives and our future.

My History Is America's History will help make our nation's celebration of the new millennium a time that reveals and enriches the spirit of millions of Americans. I encourage you to use the inspiration, guidance, and resources offered through **My History** to begin exploring your family's story because your history *is* America's history.

Hillary Rodham Clinton

5

15 things you can do to save

America

Follow your family's history and you will discover America's history.

1 Keeping a journal

Start small.

Keep it fun.

Write a little

bit every day

if you can.

If one of your parents had written a journal, wouldn't you want to read it? Do your children and grandchildren a favor, keep a journal yourself. Write your own personal history, what you think and feel. But be sure to write a few lines on what you see, read, and hear about—weddings, jobs, scandals, local news, politics, parades. All these things are American history in the making.

If you don't know where to start, look in a library or bookstore for books on keeping a journal or writing an autobiography. One piece of advice appears in nearly all these sources—relax. Start small. Keep it fun. Write a little bit every day if you can. Years from now you will have a document that will amaze you, fascinate your descendants, and show connections you never suspected to other parts of your family history and the nation's. ★

Below and right: **The cover and first page of William Swain's journal.**
Facing page: **Frederick Granger Williams, Rebecca Swain Williams, and a letter from William Swain to his wife, Sabrina.**

The Property of
William Swain
Youngstown
Niagara Co
N. Y.

April 11th 1849

Journal of Rout to
Calafornia from my
Home in Youngstown
Via of Buffal, Detroit
Chicaugo St Louis &
Indipendance: Commencing
April 11th 1849.
All my things being ready
on last night I rose early &
commenced packing them in my
trunk preparatory to leaving home,
on my long journey. leaving
for the first time my home &
dear friends with the prospect of
abscent from them for many
months & pehaps year
Among these were, an affeclion
wife to whom I have been Marred
leß than two year, an infant

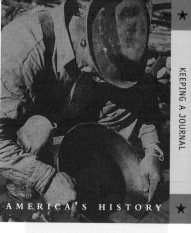
The Swains' story

William Swain of Youngstown, New York, kept a journal of his trip west. For eight months he wrote almost every day, and left rich, detailed descriptions of his companions, the landscape, and the events of his journey. He also sent letters home to his wife, mother, and brother. Many of his letters and entries betray a sense of urgency—William Swain had joined the Gold Rush.

Swain's daughter Sara treasured the diary, and kept it and the letters safe for many years. In 1938, she donated the journal to Yale University. Her gift preserved the fragile document, and the story of her father's harrowing cross-country race to riches that he never found. She later agreed to part with the letters between her parents, William and Sabrina. Their correspondence is filled with hope, the ache of separation, and deep religious faith. Like the journal, the letters are filled with American history—Sabrina's daily life on a farm in rural New York and William's days on the trail, in the mining camps, and aboard ship on the way home. Historian J. S. Holliday made the journal and the family's letters the heart of his book *The World Rushed In: The California Gold Rush Experience.*

As the journal weaves among the threads of American history, it nearly intersects the story of another Swain's journey west. In 1815, Rebecca Swain, William's sister, married Frederick Granger Williams, who became a counselor to Joseph Smith, founder of The Church of Jesus Christ of Latter-day Saints, better know as the Mormons. Eleven years before her brother went west, Rebecca Swain Williams and her husband followed Joseph Smith into the frontier states of Missouri and Illinois. They endured different hardships on their journey, as religious persecution cost Smith his life and drove the Mormons

across the Midwest to their haven in the Salt Lake Valley in 1847.

William Swain's journal shows that he passed within 100 miles of his sister near the end of August 1849. Neither may have known the other was anywhere near. Each was on his or her own path, and each part of a larger current of American history that would transform the West. But some 150 years later, their descendants made up for the missed opportunity with a reunion of their own.

One thread of the Swain family story leads to Velma Skidmore, the great-great granddaughter of Frederick Williams and Rebecca Swain. With the help of many relatives, she organized a gathering for both sides of the family that included trips to the original Williams homestead in Newburgh, Ohio, and the cobblestone home built in 1836 by Isaac Swain, William and Rebecca's father, in Youngstown, New York. The people at that reunion were living proof of the connections between family history and American history. Their ancestors were the characters of William Swain's journal, the recipients of his letters, the founding families of the Mormon Church, and some of the first families of Youngstown, New York, and Newburgh, Ohio. Their joint family website is at users.sisna.com/jfarr. A debt to William Swain also links them, for his patience and determination, just to keep a journal.

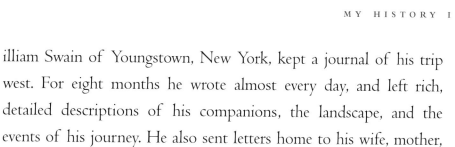

STEAMO

Mrs. Sabrina Swain
Youngstown
Niagara Co
New York

1799
Velma Skidmore's great-great-great-grandfather William Wheeler Williams establishes a township near present-day Cleveland, Ohio.

1805
Velma's great-great-great-grandfather Isaac Swain settles in Youngstown, New York, near Lake Ontario.

1815
Velma's great-great-grandmother Rebecca Swain, daughter of Isaac, marries Frederick Granger Williams, son of William Wheeler Williams.

1830
Rebecca and Frederick Williams become Mormons and follow Joseph Smith into Missouri and Illinois in search of a place to practice their religion freely.

1847
William Swain, brother of Rebecca, marries Sabrina Barrett.

1848
Reports begin to spread of the discovery of gold at Sutter's Mill, near present-day Sacramento, California.

April 11, 1849
William Swain leaves New York State to find gold and begins his diary. His path passes within 100 miles of his sister on her way to Utah.

1849
San Francisco grows from 6,000 to 15,000 residents in four months' time.

November 14, 1849
William Swain arrives in the Sierra mining camps, approximately 125 miles from San Francisco.

November 6, 1850
Unsuccessful in the mines, William Swain begins a seaward journey home with little gold or cash to show for his year in California.

February 6, 1851
William Swain arrives in Youngstown, New York, where he remains for the rest of his life.

Why family recollections matter

Tape recordings preserve your relatives' voices, how they express themselves, who they are.

Lots of people have a grandparent or a cousin who has been promising for years to write down his or her memories. Don't wait for them, and risk losing part of your family history. Interview your relatives, write down their answers, or better yet record them on tape. They will prob-ably interpret your request for an interview as an honor. Your time and effort prove that you take their memories seriously.

Conduct the interviews with a little care, and you'll end up with a coherent oral history rather than random reminiscences. The tapes will also preserve something fragile and precious—your narrators' voices, how they express themselves, a sense of who they are. The tips on page 12 will get you started. ★

For more information about conducting and preserving oral histories, use your library and visit Baylor University's Institute for Oral History's "Workshop on the Web": **www.baylor.edu/ ~Oral_History/Family.html.**

Tell your favorite family story at **www.myhistory.org**

Top: **Thelma Curley.**
Right: **Recording an oral history.**

T.W. Ransom

Dick Curley's story

MY HISTORY IS AMERICA'S HISTORY

Jerry Curley didn't know much about his father's past, and, like many fathers, Dick Curley never had much time or inclination to talk about himself. In 1992, a tragic coincidence brought Dick Curley's history to his son.

That summer, Jerry Curley joined the Southwest Memories Project, which offered workshops in interviewing and oral history. The same year, Dick Curley was diagnosed with cancer. Jerry had a few months to create a record of his father's life. Dick had a chance to preserve part of his history, his family's and his people's—the Navajo.

Jerry knew some of the details of his father's life. Dick Curley was born in Canyon Diablo, west of Winslow, Arizona, in 1927. His name was Tsish Chillie Tso, which means "Big Curly Hair." He took the name Dick Curley later, when government census takers could not say or spell his Navajo name. Dick Curley and Thelma Thompson married in the 1940s, a match arranged by their families. He worked in a munitions plant in World War II. After the war, there were few jobs on the reservation. In 1952, Dick Curley signed on as a laborer for the Santa Fe Railroad.

Jerry's interviews with his father gave him more than the facts. They gave him a feeling for his father's life and for his great strength of will:

I was determined to find work. I didn't have anything to offer my children. Even though the work didn't pay much I have followed it for forty years. . . . I obtained many things from my work, like a vehicle, sheep, cattle, and a home. Things I could call my own. This is why I followed my job.

Dick Curley had never been to school; Jerry's older brothers read road signs to him and taught him how to write his name. Yet among Navajos, he was active in tribal politics, well-respected, and known as a Haataali, or Singer, and as Hastiin Ayoyalti, "the man who could speak," because of his strong opinions and eloquent speeches. He told his children to take advantage of the white man's education but to keep Navajo culture and language. The combination, he said, would be very powerful.

Jerry, in his way, has followed his father's advice ever since. The sessions with his father led to a larger project interviewing Navajo railroad workers across the Southwest. He learned about the changes in their lives and jobs over the years and sometimes about their memories of his father. No one in the union worked for the railroad longer, and more than one worker described him as a man who was never afraid to speak his mind. Jerry Curley's oral history rescued his father's pride in his culture and his life's work. "I was at the top of the seniority list," Dick Curley told his son, "Number one."

1927
Tsish Chillie Tso (Big Curly Hair) is born and later given the name Dick Curley.

About 1938
After the death of his father, Dick Curley takes over sheep tending and other aspects of his family's farm.

About 1942
Dick Curley marries Thelma Thompson, a match arranged by their parents.

About 1943
Dick and Thelma Curley move to Barstow, California, where Dick works in a munitions plant.

1945
Navajo begin leaving the reservation in large numbers, looking for wage work.

1947–1948
Severe winter brings national attention to living conditions of Navajo and Hopi. In its aftermath, the Bureau of Indian Affairs establishes a job relocation program.

1952
Dick Curley begins working on the Santa Fe Railroad.

1956
Jerry Curley born.

1960
The Curleys acquire their first television.

1992
Dick Curley retires from the railroad; Jerry Curley begins oral history.

1993
Dick Curley passes away.

Above: **The remains of the Curley "section house" in Seligman, Arizona, originally provided by the Santa Fe Railroad.** Left: **Dick and Thelma Curley, 1952.**

Top: **Dick Curley.**
Left: **Dick Curley, second from left in the top row, with his railroad crew.**

How to do an interview

The most important piece of advice is simple: get started. Your family history isn't getting any younger. And at the beginning, think about the end. You want to finish with balanced portraits of family members in a logical collection of good-quality recordings that your grandchildren can make sense of 50 years from now.

Before the interview

- Pick a good candidate. Older relatives are obvious choices, but you might want to start with the one you're most comfortable with.

- Do a little research. Learn when and where your narrator was born, a few facts about his or her parents, spouse, children, occupation, and community, and create a simple information sheet. Then visit a library and look over books, a timeline, an encyclopedia, or videotapes about American history. The more you know about your narrator's times, the richer the interview.

- Get in touch early—give your narrator time to get ready for the interview. Explain why you are conducting the interview and what you plan to do with the notes and tapes.

- Buy, borrow, or rent a reliable tape recorder and learn how to use it. Find one with an external microphone—the sound will be better. Run the recorder from a power cord, or bring extra batteries.

The questions

- Give your interview a focus—you will overwhelm yourself and your relatives if the subject is "life."

- Ask yourself what you really want to know about the person before you begin, then give some thought to what might interest your narrator most. If you make sure the first interview is fun, chances are you can arrange another, and you will want to.

- Make broad categories of questions—family life and relationships; the narrator's life in the community; his or her reaction to important historical events. Make a list of topics and subtopics and bring it to the interview. A few specific questions prepared beforehand will also help get the interview going. Most libraries and bookstores have books with sample questions.

The interview

- Be sure the recorder is working properly. Start by recording the narrator's name, the date, place, your name, and the general subject of the interview.

- Ask open-ended questions. If you say "Tell me about your first job" or "What was it like to grow up with ten brothers and sisters?" you give the narrator a chance to explore his or her memories.

- After you ask a question, let the narrator talk. Relax and listen. Don't interrupt.

- Take notes and ask follow-up questions. If your narrator touches on an area of interest, say "Tell me more" or "Can you give me an example?" Don't be afraid to stray from your list of topics and questions.

- Be encouraging and considerate. Don't pry. Interviews sometimes touch on sensitive or painful subjects. Give your narrator the chance to drop an uncomfortable subject or to gather himself or herself in silence for a few moments. Let the tape run. The silences can be meaningful, too.

- Don't be too timid. You can ask difficult questions if you have a good reason, just ask politely. And don't take sides. Different members of your family will remember things differently. Your job is to record a thoughtful oral history, not to confirm or undercut someone's recollections or point of view.

- At the end, check over your list of topics. Go back if you've missed anything important.

- Keep the interviews to a reasonable length, especially with older narrators. Between one and two hours is usually about right.

After the interview

- Label every tape immediately. Review them as soon as you can and make a simple index by noting the subjects on the tape every five minutes or so. You can use the counter on the tape recorder to note the location of topics or particularly wonderful answers.

- Transcriptions can take a lot of time, but might be worth the investment, especially if the interviews will become part of a larger family history.

- File the tapes with the index, your information sheet about each narrator, and your notes.

- Send a thank-you note to the narrator and include a copy of the tape.

- Make sure you get a written release from the narrator, even if you only plan to use a small part of the oral history in a school paper and especially if the tapes may end up in a library or historical society.

The last word

Don't stop with one interview. Keep going. You will see American history in a new way, and create an archive of recollections that your family will be delighted to have.

Sample questions

Thinking up questions for an oral history usually isn't a problem. Choosing among them is more difficult. Here are three broad topics and a few examples of questions. Tailor your questions to your narrator.

Don't stop with one interview. Keep going.

Historical events and eras

- What is the first important event in American history that you lived through? What did you think when you heard about it?

- What do you remember about the years just after World War II?

- What is your most powerful memory of the 1960s? What did you think of the changes in the United States during that decade?

Your community

- What was your first job in your chosen occupation and where did you live at the time? What was a typical day like at work?

- Who were your neighbors and what do you remember about the neighborhood you lived in?

- What was your town like?

Your family

- What did your parents expect of you (behavior, chores, work, school)?

- What was the best time for you in your family, and the roughest time?

- Who was included in your "immediate" family? Stepbrothers and sisters, grandparents, boarders, live-in companions, old family friends you called "aunt" or "uncle"?

- How was your family like other families, and how was it different?

3 Playing detective with photographs

Ask five questions
about your
family photos:
who, what,
where, when,
and why.

Talk to your relatives who appear in family photographs and ask them the five questions: who, what, where, when, and why. Write down their answers. If you know how a photograph connects to other information about your family, such as diaries, letters, and interviews, jot that down, too (but don't write on the photograph).

Some photographs will leave you with guesses, hunches, and new mysteries rather than answers. Save the mysteries, too. The answers might lie somewhere else in your family history. To learn how to protect your photos, turn to "Saving Your Family Treasures" on page 53. ★

A picture is supposedly worth a thousand words—what do you think this picture says?

Who appears in the photograph—a family, co-workers, strangers? Why do you think so?

Post a family photo via
www.myhistory.org

When and where do you think the photograph was taken? How can you tell?

What relationships do you see among the people pictured?

Discovering clues in family papers

4

War, peace, love, death, recipes, and weather reports—this is the stuff old family letters and diaries are made of. They will show you both sides of your family history, remarkable and ordinary. Letters or diaries of relatives long gone carry fragments of their ideas and their point of view, as well as a glimpse of their times.

Family Bibles sometimes have lists of relatives stretching back for generations. Diplomas, invitations, newspaper clippings, and ticket stubs also hold part of your family's story. A little detective work will reveal how these paper treasures fit into your family history, and a little care can preserve them.

Try to identify the writer and recipient of family letters, as well as when and where they were written. Some may be hard to read or written in a foreign language. A transcription or translation can help. Write down as much as you can find out about the organizations and events represented by other records and mementos. As you fill in the gaps between these paper records, they will help fill in the gaps in your family history. ★

A little detective
work will reveal
how paper
treasures fit into
your family history.

Sallie Walton's story

MY HISTORY IS AMERICA'S HISTORY

Angela Walton's great-grandmother Sallie passed away in 1961, when Angela was 9 years old. Her father inherited Sallie Walton's Bible. Inside was a sheet of paper that Angela occasionally unfolded and studied, especially when someone brought up the subject of "Indian blood" in the family. The paper showed the boundaries of a township and bore the words "Choctaw Nation" and "Sallie Walton." Another note in the Bible had Sallie's name, a number, and a mysterious abbreviation, "Choc. Fr." But no one in the family knew the meaning of the second note, nor much about Angela's great-grandmother or her background.

Clues in family papers

Top: **Sallie Walton.**
Right: **Samuel and Sallie Walton.**

Agents of the Dawes
Commission interview
applicants to determine
land allotments.

Angela Walton grew up in Arkansas, not far from the Oklahoma border. In the summer, her family piled into the car and headed west to visit her cousins, aunts, uncles, and great-grandmother. As they crossed the Arkansas River, her father would point to a sign on the bridge that said "Entering Indian Territory," and Angela would feel a little rush of mystery and excitement. Present-day Oklahoma was once set aside as permanent territory for American Indians, before it was opened to white settlement in the 1880s. "You know, Nannie is Indian," her father always added, "she's a Choctaw."

Nannie was Sallie Walton. On visits to her home, Angela spent hot summer days racing around with her cousins and quieter moments listening to the reminiscences of her relatives— elderly black men and women recalling their lives growing up in Arkansas and Oklahoma. She understood that her great-grandmother was connected to the Choctaws, and that she must be connected to them, too. Some of her friends at school bragged about being related to Cherokees chiefs. But to Angela, the talk about Indians in her family never meant much. The Indians she knew best fought cowboys and lived on television.

Over the years, Angela Walton grew more interested in family history and signed up for classes on genealogy. She also married and moved to Maryland, near Washington, D.C. In 1991,

thirty years after she lost her great-grandmother, Angela Walton-Raji found her again— down the hall from the Constitution, not far from the Declaration of Independence, at the National Archives.

Angela Walton-Raji had learned that records about the Indians of Oklahoma were on microfilm at the Archives. One day she stopped by and started looking through the reels of film, but without success. Then recalling the note about "Choc. Fr.," and realizing for the first time that it stood for Choctaw Freedmen, she turned to the microfilm labeled Freedmen Records. On the second roll, in file 777, she found her family—Samuel Walton, Sallie Walton, and their two sons and stepdaughter. Among the pages Angela copied, she later discovered the names of her great-great-grandparents, and another surprising piece of family history. Sallie's father was a Choctaw Indian named Eastman Williams. Both of Angela's great-grandparents had been born into slavery, and at one time both were enslaved by Choctaws.

Angela Walton-Raji's discovery drew her to a time and place in the nation's history that few Americans know much about. The Choctaws were one of the "Five Civilized Tribes," along with Cherokees, Chickasaws, Creeks, and Seminoles. These nations grew cotton, raised livestock, and prospered in the agricultural economy of the Southeast in the 1700s and early 1800s. From the point

of view of white settlers, the people of the five tribes were "civilized" because of their success as planters.

Presidents from Thomas Jefferson to Andrew Jackson and southern state governments were eager to promote white settlement and plantation agriculture across the South. To open all the lands east of the Mississippi River and parts of present-day Louisiana and Texas, the federal government passed the Indian Removal Act of 1830. The act forced the Five Civilized Tribes from their lands in the Southeast in return for the promise of a permanent home in present-day Oklahoma. The Choctaw left almost

immediately; some tribes resisted. But over the next decade, all but a few ultimately traveled west. On one exodus in the winter of 1837–38, thousands of Cherokees lost their lives to winter cold, starvation, and disease. Their path came to be called the Trail of Tears.

From the days when Europeans and African Americans first encountered the people of the

Above: **Angela Walton-Raji's**
book *Black Indian Genealogy*
Research, **Sallie Walton's**
Bible, and Sallie Walton and
her son.

Sallie Walton

1787
Northwest Ordinance establishes Indian nations as separate governments, nations within a nation.

1803
Thomas Jefferson purchases the Louisiana territory from Napoleon.

1830
Indian Removal Act requires the relocation of the Five Civilized Tribes from east of the Mississippi to Indian Territory, now Oklahoma. Choctaw acquiesce, whereas other tribes resist removal.

1831
Cherokee Nation takes the State of Georgia to the U.S. Supreme Court, which declines to hear case because Cherokees are considered a separate nation and not bound by U.S. laws.

1832
Supreme Court invalidates removal policy, but President Andrew Jackson continues to push Indians west.

1837–1838
Trail of Tears: Federal troops uproot 15,000 to 20,000 Cherokees, and force them on the 800-mile march to Indian Territory. One in four dies.

1840
Samuel Walton, Angela's great-grandfather, born a slave in Arkansas.

1860
Arkansas's population doubles in 20-year period to 435,000, approximately one-fourth slave.

1862
In the Civil War, seven regiments from the Five Civilized Tribes fight with the Confederacy in the Battle of Pea Ridge.

About 1862
Samuel Walton is sold to Jim Davis, a member of the Choctaw tribe.

1863
Emancipation Proclamation frees all slaves held in states in rebellion.

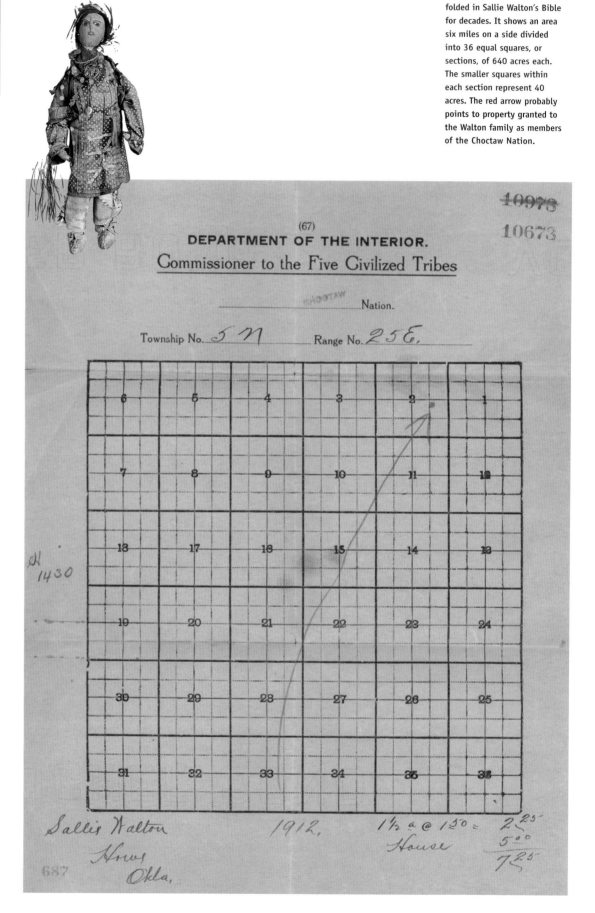

Left: **Choctaw doll.**
Below: **This township map lay folded in Sallie Walton's Bible for decades. It shows an area six miles on a side divided into 36 equal squares, or sections, of 640 acres each. The smaller squares within each section represent 40 acres. The red arrow probably points to property granted to the Walton family as members of the Choctaw Nation.**

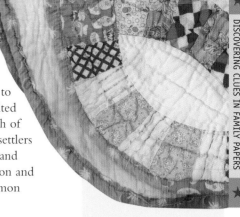

Five Civilized Tribes, some whites, blacks, and Indians formed families, and so did their "mixed-race" children. Among the peoples of the five tribes, race was often a complicated matter.

African Americans—enslaved and free—lived among the peoples of the Five Civilized Tribes in the Southeast and moved west with them. They were treated differently in different tribes. Several free black families prospered among the Creeks and Seminoles in Indian Territory. Almost none lived among the Choctaws and Chickasaws. After the Civil War, African Americans enslaved by the people of the five tribes were freed—the Waltons became Choctaw Freedmen. Like freedmen across the nation, they were seldom treated as equals. Blacks among the Choctaws were denied the right to vote in tribal affairs and shortchanged on tribal lands. To escape discrimination,

many African American freedmen in Oklahoma established their own towns, schools, and churches and were joined by freed slaves and free blacks from eastern states.

In 1887, Congress passed the Dawes Act in an attempt to help Indians become full members of American society. The act ended the legal standing of tribes as separate nations, granted Indians American citizenship, and required that most of the vast Indian territories be divided among their members and no longer held in common as tribal lands. To receive land allotments, Indian freedmen among the Five Civilized Tribes had to prove to a government commission that they were former slaves and currently tribal members. Satisfying the commission often took four or five years and generated paperwork. The records that Angela Walton-Raji found at the National Archives

were part of the proof for Samuel and Sallie Walton. The rest of the tribal lands were opened to homesteaders, which ignited the Oklahoma Land Rush of 1889. As waves of white settlers arrived in the late 1800s and early 1900s, the segregation and discriminatory laws common elsewhere in the South multiplied in Oklahoma.

As Angela Walton-Raji discovered, the Dawes Commission records are a reservoir of clues for family historians with Native American roots. Some 20,000 freedmen are listed on the rolls. Since many of the records name previous owners of enslaved African Americans, they give some families a rare chance to trace their ancestors to the years before the Civil War. Angela Walton-Raji's search for her family history turned on just such a piece of evidence, and on two sheets of paper in a Bible. These documents—and all she learned in making sense of them —also gave her a deeper under- standing of the complexities of race in American history, and the chance to help other family historians with her book, *Black Indian Genealogy Research,* and website: members.aol.com/ angelaw859/index.html

1863
Angela's great-grandmother Sallie Anchatubbe born a slave of Emaline Perry, a Choctaw.

1865
Thirteenth Amendment abolishes slavery throughout the United States, but not in Indian Territory.

1866
Slaves among Five Civilized Tribes are freed by treaty with U.S. government. Sallie and Sam Walton go free.

1887
Dawes Act brings tribal nations into the United States and awards land to members of Indian nations, including freedmen.

1889
Oklahoma Land Rush.

1890–1910
African Americans establish a dozen towns across Oklahoma.

1899
Sam and Sallie Walton testify before a federal commission to support their application for a land allotment.

1907
Oklahoma, home to 20,000 freedmen, admitted as a state.

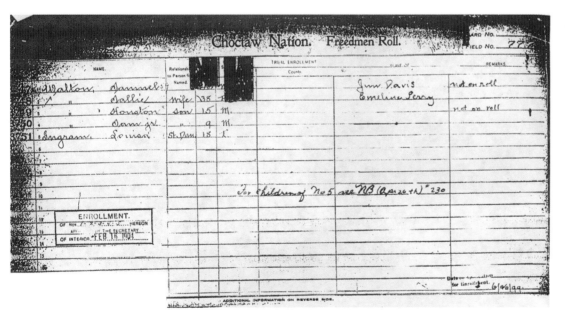

Top: **Detail of a quilt made by Sallie Walton.**
Above left: **Slave house on a plantation near Talala, Indian Territory, 1900.**

Left: **The enrollment card for the Walton family lists members of the family at left and their former owners on the right.**

Uncovering history in the attic

Clothing, silver, furniture, and works of art make the journey from one generation to the next. But the stories that help give meaning to these treasures often don't survive the trip. Ask family members about their possessions from the past, the original owner, and special stories or memories about each item. Incorporate their answers into a family history.

Your local library or historical society will have books and articles on historic decor, furnishings, clothing, and other artifacts so you can learn more about the history of your heirlooms and how to protect them. The section of this guidebook on "Saving Your Family Treasures" will also help.

If you come across an unusual item, ask a curator or other expert at a museum or historical society for more information. ★

Ask family members about possessions from the past.

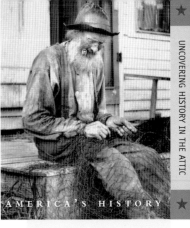

The Morses' story

M arie Locke's family history was safe in the attic, in her grand-mother's memory, and in her great-grandfather's greatest passion, photography. The attic was in the home of her grandmother, Irene Morse Bartlett, who lived in the village of Islesford on Little Cranberry Island off the coast of Maine from 1909 to 1998. The treasures overhead had held Marie's curiosity since childhood, and her summers spent exploring the island included many special afternoons in the attic.

She had always known about her great-grandfather Fred Morse's turn-of-the-century photographs. She eventually decided to ask her grandmother to tell her the story behind the photographs and gather some of the images and recollections into a simple family history book. Not long after, on a visit to the island, a friend of Marie's, designer Nancy Montgomery, saw some of the images and suggested a more elaborate possibility. That weekend was the start of a five-year project to create a book that would paint a picture of early island life through the eyes of Irene Morse Bartlett and her photographer father Fred.

The project began with Irene's daughter Jo bringing down from the attic a cardboard box full of Fred's glass-plate negatives wrapped in newspaper. Irene held the plates up to the light from the window and described what she saw. As the stories unfolded, Jo retrieved more objects from the attic and Marie, her grand-mother, and Nancy Montgomery went over them one by one.

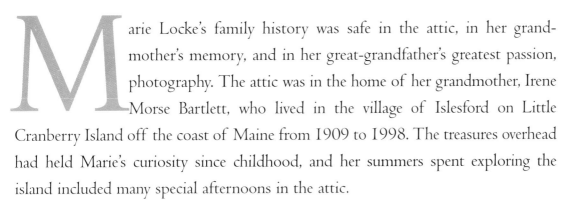

Many of the treasures from the attic were old merchandise from the family's general store. A glass ladle with a small hole in the bottom was a pickle dipper for scooping pickles from a barrel. The lid of a crate for Goudy and Kent's Biscuits declared the contents "Best on the Land" and "Best on the Sea." A flared Moxie glass came from the makers of Moxie, the first mass-marketed soft drink in the country, still available today in New England. The drink had enough kick to produce a slang term for pluck and boldness, namely "moxie." Irene's attic also produced lamb's wool soles for soft slippers, metal disks called Mendets to mend pots and pans, and buttons made of bone and buffalo horn. Marie's grandmother remembered something about all of them and what they revealed about everyday life on the island.

Some of the keepsakes from the attic were personal, not commercial. There were quill pens from Irene's school days. From a church fair, someone had saved a pillow made of ribbons used to tie bundles of tobacco. Irene still had the head of a doll that

1870
Marie Locke's great grandfather Fred Morse is born in Maine.

1885
Orphaned at age 11, Fred Morse eventually arrives on Little Cranberry Island to work as a fish skinner.

1893
Mary Smyth, who will become Fred's second wife, emigrates during a year when arrivals from Ireland number nearly 43,600—10 percent of all immigrants.

1894
Fred Morse and Fanny Stanley marry.

1897
Tourism increases on the island, as professors, doctors, and their families travel by boat from Boston to spend their summer there.

1900
Mary Smyth works for Boston families. Half of Irish-born women living in Massachusetts work as household servants.

Top: **Mending a net.**
Above: **Tourists by the surf, about 1900.**
Left: **Fred Morse's camera.**

1903

Fanny Stanley dies of tuberculosis.

1906

Mary Smyth arrives at Little Cranberry Island working as a nanny for a summer family and meets Fred Morse. At the end of the summer, Mary returns to Boston and Fred travels to the mainland to pursue a career in photography. He survives the San Francisco earthquake.

1907

Mary Smyth and Fred Morse marry in Boston and settle in Greenville, South Carolina; Fred works at a photographic studio.

1909

Irene Morse is born.

1909

Nathan Stanley asks Fred Morse to run the general store. The Morse family moves back to Islesford.

1917

First motor vehicle brought to island on barge.

1950

Morse general store destroyed in fire.

came all the way from France, and would have had the rest if she hadn't left the doll on the lawn one day when her father was mowing. She had also saved some sweetgrass baskets made by John Snow, a Passamaquoddy Indian. In the summer he traveled around the islands selling his baskets to the residents and the steadily growing number of tourists.

None of the other heirlooms in the attic, however, could quite match Fred's photographs. His images showed the island through the years, from portraits of the Morse family to sailboats in the harbor. The old schoolhouse, the general store, sea views, landscapes, a frozen harbor, and panoramas of the village of Islesford are among Morse's images. By themselves, the pictures preserve a portion of small-town life in the early 1900s. Their creator was an accomplished photographer and a shopkeeper, actor, father, orphan, and soda jerk. His life on Little Cranberry Island is partly a story of how families and family history are built from bonds of affection, not just blood.

Fred Morse came to the island as a teenager in 1885 to find work as a fish skinner. There he met Fannie Stanley, the only child of Margaret and Nathan Stanley. The Stanleys were descendants of one of the first families to settle the island in the 1700s. In 1894, Fannie and Fred married, and the couple moved in with Fannie's parents. Fred painted houses in nearby Bar Harbor for a time. He later opened a soda fountain in the Hotel Islesford. But the Morses were married only nine years. Fannie died of tuberculosis in 1903, and Fred set out across the United States.

After studying at Eppingham College of Photography in Illinois, Fred traveled to San Francisco, and survived the earthquake there in 1906. But he seemed to have left his heart in Islesford. Mary Smyth, an Irish immigrant and a nanny who came to the island with a family from Boston, had met Fred before he left. In 1907, they were married and moved to Greenville, South Carolina, where Fred set up a photography studio.

Since Fannie's death, Fred had kept in touch with Nathan and Margaret Stanley. When the Stanleys wanted help to run the

Top: **Fred Wesley Morse.**
Right: **The Stanley and Morse family general store.**

22

general store in Islesford, they asked him to bring his family back. In 1909, Fred and Mary Morse and their infant daughter Irene moved to Little Cranberry Island to make, with the Stanleys, three generations of a new family. Irene would live on the island for nearly 90 years, and all her life thought of the Stanleys as her grandparents.

Irene Morse Bartlett's memories of the island knit together her father's photographs and the contents of her attic into a family history and nearly a century of local history on Little Cranberry Island. Tourists started coming to the island about the turn of the century, Irene told her granddaughter. They stayed at the Hotel Isleford and hired lobstermen to take them sailing on day trips. As the summer trade picked up, many families on the island rented their homes to tourists and lived in their sheds for the season. Irene remembered selling milk to the natives for 12 cents and to the summer visitors for 20, "the only double standard we had." Her mother, she recalled, helped out in the store, raised children, and played basketball with a group of ladies who scandalized the island by wearing bloomers on the court. She also wrote local gossip and

news for the *Bar Harbor Times*. Irene started ghostwriting the column for her mother in the 1930s, and carried on until 1998, when her daughter Jo took over.

During World War II, the U.S. government inadvertently contributed to the family's history by establishing a tax on the inventories of general stores like the Morse's. The family took part of their goods and hid

them in the attic of their home, across the street. Then on New Year's Day in 1950, Mary Morse accidentally burned the general store to the ground while cleaning out the woodburning stove. The cracker boxes, ribbons, root beer extract, and all the other goods were safe across the street for Marie Locke to discover and years later weave into the story of her family and a book, *Memories of a Maine Island*.

For a closer look at *Memories of a Maine Island: Turn of the Century Tales and Photographs* by Marie Locke and Nancy Montgomery, visit www.memoriesofmaine.com

Top left: **Eight young fish skinners on Little Cranberry Island. Fred Morse is in the bottom row, at the left.**
Top right: **Mary Smyth Morse and child.**
Right: **Boys by the water in Islesford, Little Cranberry Island, 1900.**

6 Exploring your home's history

Houses are an expression of the people who lived in them and their times.

Like a family photograph or an old letter, your home is evidence about your history, especially if it has remained in the family for a few generations. Houses are an expression of the people who lived in them and their times. Apartment buildings reveal trends in architecture and building construction. Fixtures, landscaping, and the size of rooms are tied up with tastes in architecture and technologies such as air conditioning and lawn mowers. An addition to a home might offer clues about births, new jobs, and the local economy. Nearly 43 million Americans move every year, and a few of those moves might have generated documents that can help in your search.

Getting started is easy. Write down what you know and go from there—when you bought your home or when you moved in; who lives there now. Then start working back.

Exploring a home's history means a trip to the city or county courthouse to look at deeds, title documents, building plans, permits, and other public records. A historical society, your neighbors, and the local history section of your public library are likely sources, too.

With any luck, you will learn who owned your house or building and when, and perhaps how its appearance has changed over the years. You might find that you have led

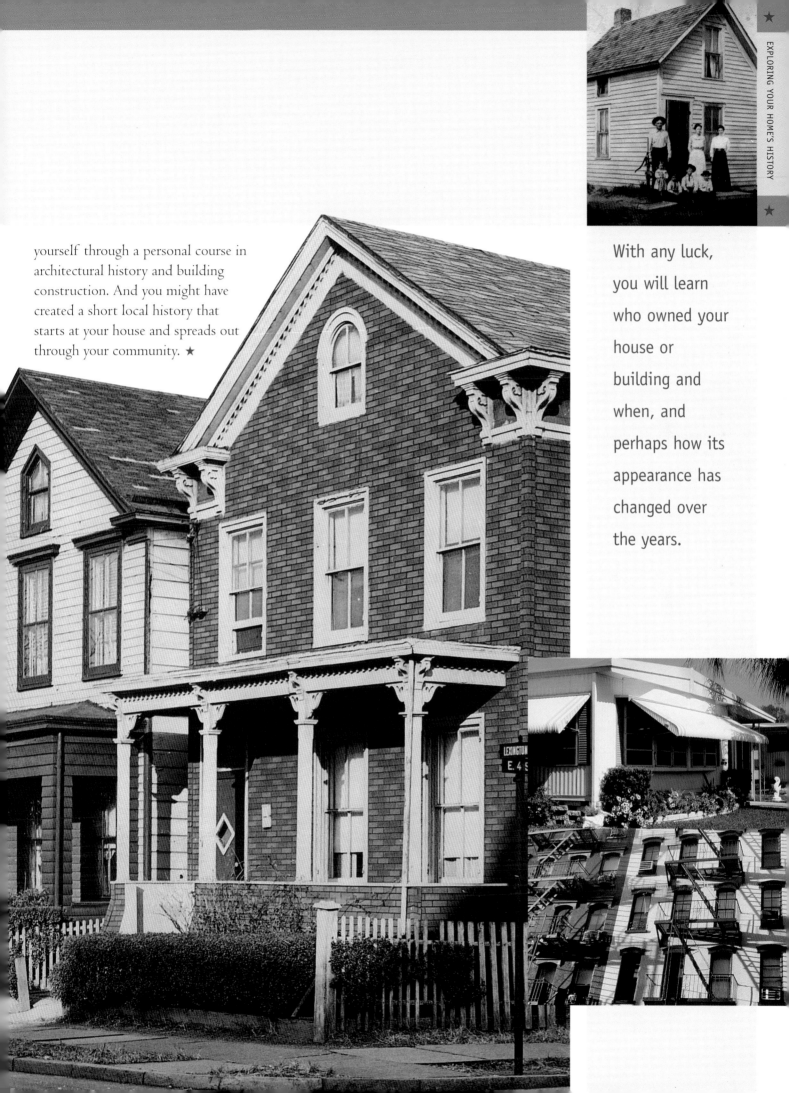

yourself through a personal course in architectural history and building construction. And you might have created a short local history that starts at your house and spreads out through your community. ★

With any luck, you will learn who owned your house or building and when, and perhaps how its appearance has changed over the years.

7 Climbing the family tree

Research your ancestors—try a little genealogy.

If family history brings out the detective in you, don't stop at interviewing your relatives. Investigate your ancestors—try a little genealogy. The job still involves collecting facts and anecdotes about your relatives, but as you go back through the generations, the mysteries grow and you rely on different evidence.

Birth certificates, marriage records, and other legal documents can give you the official information about family members. Be sure to include records for yourself. Federal and state censuses offer clues about the movement of your family members between states, occupations, even nations. Visit county courthouses to look at records of land exchanges, wills, and probate records. Local cemeteries can also help reveal family ties.

Keep track of all your sources of information carefully, including correspondence. Make a record of what you find—and what you don't.

To learn more about genealogical research, visit your local library, call your local or state historical society, check in the yellow pages for a genealogical organization near you, or write to the National Genealogical Society at 4527 N. 17th Street, Arlington, VA 22207-2399 ★

The World Wide Web has a wealth of resources. The NEH does not make endorsements, but here are a few places you can go online to get started.

"The Genealogy Page" of the National Archives and Records Administration	**www.nara.gov/genealogy/genindex.html**
The National Genealogical Society	**www.ngsgeneaology.org**
Genealogy.com	**www.genealogy.com**
Cyndi's List	**www.cyndislist.com**
USGenWeb Project's Information for Researchers	**www.usgenweb.org**
Family Search Internet Genealogy Service	**www.FamilySearch.com**
MyFamily.com	**www.myfamily.com**

★ To discover connections between your history and the nation's, visit the My History website at: **www.myhistory.org**

Right: **Julia Fong's family tree. Her family history appears on page 49.**

Four Generations of a Family Tree

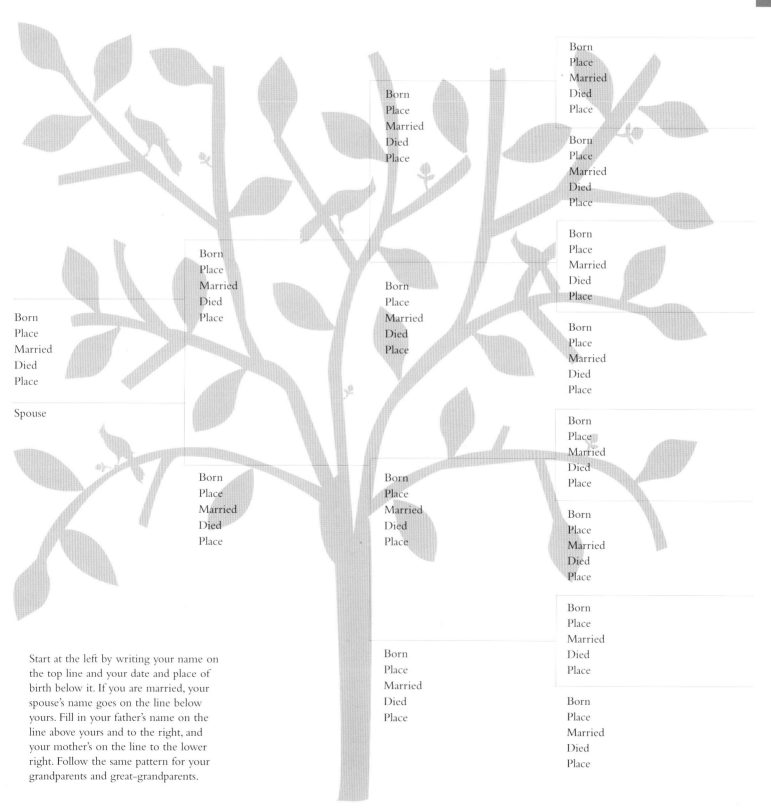

Born
Place
Married
Died
Place

Born
Place
Married
Died
Place

Born
Place
Married
Died
Place

Born
Place
Married
Died
Place

Born
Place
Married
Died
Place

Born
Place
Married
Died
Place

Born
Place
Married
Died
Place

Born
Place
Married
Died
Place

Born
Place
Married
Died
Place

Born
Place
Married
Died
Place

Born
Place
Married
Died
Place

Born
Place
Married
Died
Place

Born
Place
Married
Died
Place

Born
Place
Married
Died
Place

Spouse

Start at the left by writing your name on the top line and your date and place of birth below it. If you are married, your spouse's name goes on the line below yours. Fill in your father's name on the line above yours and to the right, and your mother's on the line to the lower right. Follow the same pattern for your grandparents and great-grandparents.

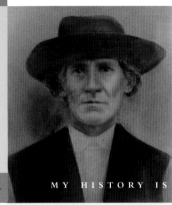

CLIMBING THE FAMILY TREE

The Madrids' story

MY HISTORY IS AMERICA'S HISTORY

Tom Madrid ultimately discovered the first ancestor bearing his family name to set foot in the United States—Francisco de Madrid. He was a wagon driver, or *chirrionero de los carros*. On his journey north from Mexico, he traveled with ten soldiers and four Catholic missionaries along a twisting, rocky road that ran beside the Rio Grande. They reached the small settlement of San Gabriel, in present-day New Mexico, in 1603.

Top: **Juan Antonio Madrid, Tom Madrid's great-great-grandfather, about 1883.**
Right: **The signature of Roque de Madrid, Tom Madrid's 7th great-grandfather.**

The mission at San Juan Pueblo, an early Spanish settlement in New Mexico.

When Francisco de Madrid arrived in New Mexico, the Spanish colony there was barely five years old, and struggling to survive. It had been founded by Juan de Oñate in 1598—nine years before English settlers arrived at Jamestown. Francisco de Madrid, his sons, and grandsons married the daughters and granddaughters of some of the original settlers, such as Gerónimo Márquez. These men, their wives, and children joined the ongoing struggle between native peoples who had inhabited the continent for thousands of years and new arrivals from Europe. For them it was daily life.

The life of Tom's ancestor Gerónimo Márquez, one of Juan de Oñate's trusted captains, reveals some of the hardships of the times. In September 1598, Oñate ordered Márquez and four other soldiers to track down deserters from the colony who were headed back to Mexico. They caught up to the runaways and executed two of them on the spot. Two months later, Márquez was part of a hurried retreat from the Acoma Pueblo after Indians killed the leader of his party and several other soldiers. In January 1599, he returned as part of a force that killed and captured hundreds of Acomas in retaliation. In 1604-05, he was a member of an expedition led by Oñate to the Gulf of California; the party survived the return trip by eating their horses.

About 1609, the Spanish colonists in New Mexico moved some 25 miles south from San Gabriel to a narrow valley that they thought would be easier to defend. They established a new settlement there, the city of Holy Faith, or Santa Fe. Francisco de Madrid, Gerónimo Márquez, and other ancestors of Tom Madrid were among the original residents. Today, their tiny walled village is the oldest capital city in the United States.

Poverty, hunger, desertions, and conflicts between the clergy, the military, and political leaders plagued the colony. For the next 70 years, the fortunes of Tom Madrid's ancestors rose and fell in the turbulent history of Santa Fe and New Mexico. In 1640, several of Tom Madrid's relatives joined a plot against the Spanish governor, Luis de Rosas, who was eventually assassinated in 1642. Two were beheaded for their part in the affair, including Diego Márquez, the son of Gerónimo.

Less than 40 years later, the native peoples of the region rose up in the Pueblo Revolt and drove the Spanish out of New Mexico. Roque de Madrid, Francisco's grandson, was one of the colonists who fled down the Rio Grande with his family. Twelve years later he returned as a lieutenant to Diego de Vargas, the military leader who reconquered the region for Spain.

The Madrids

Piecing together his family history took Tom Madrid more than a decade. He found inspiration for the work on the other side of his family, in his maternal grandfather. In 1984, when Sabino Vialpando died at age

92, his grandson Tom was left with question after question for his grandfather, all too late to ask. "Looking back," he said, "I think my initial interest in finding out about my heritage was to preserve his memory."

Top: **Madrid Plaza, in Madrid, Colorado, built in 1862.**
Above left: **Clorinda Madrid, Tom Madrid's grandmother.**
Above: **Sabino Vialpando, Tom's maternal grandfather, in World War I uniform.**
Left: **Wedding day of great aunt Jesusita Vialpando and Juan Mestas.**

1540–41
The search for the mythical Seven Cities of Cibola brings Spanish explorers to the Southwest, among them Francisco Vásquez de Coronado.

1598
Juan de Oñate establishes towns for Spain in present-day New Mexico, including San Gabriel and San Juan. San Juan Bautista founded as a Spanish mission for Pueblo Indians. Tom Madrid's 10th great-grandfather, Gerónimo Márquez, serves with Oñate.

1603
Tom Madrid's 9th great-grandfather, Francisco de Madrid, arrives at San Gabriel.

1607
On the eastern coast of the United States, Jamestown, Virginia, becomes the first permanent settlement by English colonists.

1607–1610
Spanish found Santa Fe, the capital of New Mexico. Members of Madrid family settle there. Colonists and Indian laborers construct the Palace of the Governors, Las Casas Reales.

1680
The Pueblo Revolt drives the Spanish from New Mexico.

1692–96
Tom Madrid's 7th great-grandfather, Roque de Madrid, takes part in the reconquest of Pueblo lands and leads an expedition into Navajo territory.

TOM'S RESEARCH LED HIM TO THE STATE ARCHIVES of New Mexico, the Catholic Church, The Church of Jesus Christ of Latter Day Saints, the National Archives and Records Administration, and county courthouses in Colorado and New Mexico. He joined the Genealogical Society of Hispanic America and traveled with his wife to many of the towns where his ancestors had lived, including one they helped found, Trinidad, Colorado. He is a self-described stickler for documentation. Any other researcher using his sources, he says, could follow his tracks and learn what he has learned. The whole remarkable chain of family history from Gerónimo Márquez and Francisco de Madrid is on the Madrid family website: www.users.uswest.net/~madridt/index.htm. But then following clues may come easier for Tom Madrid than for most people, since he is a police detective.

Finding your family's place in American history

Your great-grandmother's footprints might be on the Oregon Trail. The Civil War might have been your family's war, and the Civil Rights Movement your family's struggle for equality. Everything you have discovered about your ancestors' lives— names, dates, and movements from place to place—fits into the larger story of the nation's past. So consult timelines on American history and world history to compare important events in your family's history with regional, national, and international events. Trace your family's movements on maps, recent and historical. Let these connections lead you to books and websites that focus on the events, time periods, and geographic areas that you found in your ancestors' stories. Look at the lists of books and films beginning on page 70 for good places to start.

This broader perspective will help in your genealogical research, and it will also make your own story more meaningful to you. Follow your family's history and you will discover America's history. ★

Writing your own story

Share your family history with your family—write a story. Pick a time, a place, or a person to start with. You might focus on one especially interesting relative. Recount his or her experience of an accomplishment, a disaster, a battle, or a move across the country. Your story could begin where your family lives (or lived), and follow the family's original migration there, the conditions when they arrived, and how the people and place changed over the years.

Before you begin to write, review the information you have collected about your family and American history. Define a focus and scope for your story to help select facts to include and resist the temptation to tell everything you know. Try to accomplish two goals: tell the reader what is unique about your family and also what experiences your family shared with other people of the same era. ★

The Petersons' story

MY HISTORY IS AMERICA'S HISTORY

Logging was mostly winter work in the North Woods, and during the winter James and Anna Peterson were apart for weeks and months at a time. Their long separations were simply part of their life together. "Dear Ma," he wrote her on Easter of 1942, "When I was ready to start yesterday the horses had gone away. . . . I went out to look and it was dark before I got home with them."

Top: **Jim and Anna Peterson.**

James Peterson was a lumberjack in Wisconsin for fifty years and a roadbuilder for decades. His father, Jens, had left Denmark for the United States in the late 1800s. Jens found work with the Soo Line Railroad, which carried grain and other freight across the Upper Midwest. He made his way to Wisconsin and settled north of Medford. Like hundreds of thousands of others —immigrants and American citizens alike—he staked a claim under the Homestead Act.

Homesteaders could claim up to 160 acres of unoccupied land owned by the government if they remained on the land for five years, cultivated it, and put up a permanent structure. Jens built a shed to live in while he started his farm, constructed a log home, and lived as a farmer, fisherman, and lumberjack. Four years after he left Denmark, he sent for his wife and daughters.

Jens and his wife had three sons and another daughter in the United States. James, the oldest

son, married Anna Berg in 1907 and bought the family farm from his father. James stayed with logging, and he had a head for business. By age 18 he had saved enough money to buy his own horses and equipment. While he managed a growing crew of loggers, Anna ran the farm. Their sons, George and Morgan, were born in 1909 and 1911.

In 1928, a reporter from the Taylor County *Star News* interviewed James about his trade. "There is something about this woods that gets a man to like it," he said. "Your real lumberjack couldn't be kept out of the woods in winter. It's something more than the wages he gets out of it. Why some of the men have 12 to 15 thousand dollars cold cash in the bank— but the woods call to them and they come back." The article described life in a logging camp, including the long hours for the lumberjacks and the longer hours for the camp cook and his assistants, the "cookees." They cooked about 100 pounds of meat a day for the 105 men in James Peterson's camp—five

tons of meat for the whole season. Two tons of sugar, five tons of flour, 400 bushels of potatoes, and sacks of beans, vegetables, and other food kept the lumberjacks alive through the winter.

"Something about the woods" got to James and Anna's sons. They began logging in their teens. Like his father and grandfather, Morgan endured the ups and downs of the logging business, economic depressions, and the snow. One Thanksgiving Day, he recalled, "It snowed 30 inches. It never thawed till the 1st of February. . . . That was a bad year."

Bad years for logging and farming were uncomfortably common in Wisconsin in the 1920s and 1930s. In the warmer months, some logging equipment could be put to work building roads. The Petersons turned to road construction in the early 1920s to help make ends meet. Into the fourth generation and seventy-nine years later, five family members still run the family construction business.

1890s

Angie Peterson's great-great-grandfather Jens Peterson leaves Denmark for U.S.

1899

Height of logging boom in Wisconsin; more than 3.4 billion feet of board harvested in one year.

1907

Angie's great-grandfather James Peterson marries Anna Berg and soon purchases his father's homestead.

1911

Angie's paternal grandfather, Morgan Peterson, is born.

1913

Florence Anne Hessefort, Angie's paternal grandmother, is born.

1920

U.S. Census reports the first urban majority; 51 percent of Americans live in towns of more than 2,500 residents; 29 percent on farms.

Top: **Florence Hessefort, Angie Peterson's paternal grandmother, at age 5.**
Above: **John and Anne Sherwin Hessefort, Florence Hessefort's parents.**
Left: **Lumberjacks at a logging camp, 1908.**

The Pearsons

1929-32

With the Great Depression, farm income declines by 60 percent; one third of all farmers lose their land.

1930

Morgan and Florence marry and move in with his parents.

1933

President Franklin D. Roosevelt launches New Deal, which includes the Agricultural Adjustment Act, providing price supports for farmers.

1936

The Rural Electrification Act establishes utility cooperatives to provide electricity to rural homes.

1936

Florence and Morgan build their own home on Highway M, near Medford. Electricity comes two years later.

1980

Less than 3 percent of population lives on farms.

Above right: **Barn building in Wisconsin, 1895.**
Right: **Hauling out the logs, 1914.**

Morgan asked Florence Hessefort to a dance in April 1928, and they hit it off well enough to stay together for 60 years. Their dates included dances and ice cream sundaes, but if Morgan and Florence happened to be out at 10 p.m., they often stopped at the Medford train station. In rural Wisconsin almost seventy years ago, part of an evening's entertainment was just finding out who was coming and going. They were married on December 23, 1930. Like many families during the Great Depression, the newlyweds could not afford a home of their own. They moved in with Morgan's parents. Morgan had

34

only enough work to keep a handful of lumberjacks busy. Florence found a job as a cosmetologist and counted herself lucky.

With their first son, Jim, on the way, Florence and Morgan built their own home in 1936. But they had to wait for electricity. Electric power hadn't yet reached all the farms of Wisconsin.

As long as Morgan stayed in the logging business, he and Florence also lived through long separations. Like Anna Peterson before her, Florence ran the farm and took most of the responsibility for raising the children—three sons and a daughter by 1955. She grew vegetables, washed clothes, cooked, cleaned, made her own soap, butchered chickens, and managed the help, which at various times meant a hired man, three women, and two teenaged girls, the Grlicky sisters. Mary and Dotti Grlicky lived with the Petersons during high school and helped out on the farm so they could be close to school, which was diagonally across the road from the Petersons' farm. To feed everyone, Florence sometimes went through 50 pounds of flour a week making bread and pies and biscuits.

Jim and Anna Peterson, just married, in 1907.

Florence's journal from the year 1950 offers a glimpse of life on the farm:

Monday, February 13—
Washed clothes. Grandma and I went to see Mrs. Grlicky at hospital. Took her some jonquils.

Friday, February 17—
Cleaned house and back porch. Had French fries for supper.

Monday, July 3—
Jim and Jack went fishing with Billy Daniels while we went shopping at Hayward and looked at road job. Jackie had fish hook caught in his head above his ear. Dr. at Kateri removed it. No after effects. Took our boys and Billy to see "Sitting Pretty" movie at Hayward. Went to the Aladdin Inn later to dance and eat.

Wednesday, July 5—
Picked 6 qts strawberries at home and about 16 qts at Grandma's. Jim and Jack went fishing with Erv at night. Hauled in 4 loads hay.

Wednesday, November 30—
Pressed clothes, mended. Washed up green davenport and chair. Played cards at school card party. Morgan won 1st prize.

MORGAN AND FLORENCE'S GRANDDAUGHTER, ANGIE, began exploring the Petersons' history with a school assignment in sixth grade to make a family scrapbook. But like so many family historians, she felt a deeper need to understand her family history after the death of a relative. Her grandfather Morgan, "a walking history book," passed away over the winter holidays in 1989. In tape recordings of his stories, her grandmother's journals, the letters of James Peterson, newspaper articles, and research of her own into the logging industry, Angie Peterson found a story larger than her family's. Immigration, long separations between husbands and wives, the Great Depression, small-town romances, the rhythms of farm life, and a family's hard work and prosperity through the generations are as much a part of the nation's story as the Petersons'.

Above: **Angie Peterson and her father Terry.**
Above left: **George and Morgan Peterson, 1912.**

Fun for the family

In family history projects, your relatives can be the actors as well as the audience. The easiest way for a family historian to make his or her job easier is to get them involved. They will automatically help with research, spread the word to other family members, and lighten the workload. They will probably get caught up in the fun of family history—and history projects for the whole family, young and old, are the best way to create new family historians. Here are some projects from the editors of *FamilyFun* magazine.

Our Family Quilt

American quilts have always reflected our diverse heritage, from the simple and refined quilts of Amish communities to the crazy-patchwork quilts of early settlers. Women etched the births and deaths of family members onto quilt squares with indelible ink, then sewed them into quilts. Today, quiltmaking continues to be a creative expression of personal, family, and community history.

You can honor your own clan and create a quilt that reflects the personalities and pastimes of your family members—ask each one, young and old, to contribute a square. Your quilt can make a lovely gift to commemorate an event, such as a big wedding anniversary.

Materials
- Beginner's quilting book, if necessary
- Paper and pencil
- Four squares of prewashed, unbleached muslin per participant, cut to size
- Material of your choice for decorating each square, such as fabric paint or appliqué materials
- Cotton border, backing, and sashing, cut to size
- Cotton batting, cut to size
- Sewing supplies

1. If you or another family member is not a quilter, you can hire a professional seamstress to turn your patches into a quilt. Ask for a recommendation from your local fabric store (prices range from $10 to $15 and hour). Better yet, find out if the shop offers a quilting workshop that you could sign up for.

2. Decide how many family members you want to include in your quilt, remembering that each person will create one square. Now sketch out your quilt to see what size and shape it will be. A simple patchwork pattern in a rectangle or square is easiest.

3. Ask each participant to design one quilt square that symbolizes something special about your families, such as pictures of people, pets, houses, proverbs, family treasures, special events, or cultural symbols. Be sure to clearly outline for them the scope of the project, your goals, and your deadlines.

4. Give each participant four blank quilt squares, assuring them that you only need one to be finished and returned; the remaining squares are extras for practice or mistakes. You can also give them suggestions for techniques to use, from appliqué to photograph reproductions to fabric painting.

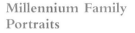

Family History Museum

Kids can investigate and then show off their family history by creating a mini-museum of prized family mementos. The exhibition hall can be a shoebox, a drawer, or a mantelpiece. When family members gather for reunions and holidays, your kids can give them tours and request donations of other important artifacts.

Materials:
• Family photos, newspaper clippings, family documents, ticket stubs from special events, and other important mementos
• A special spot for a mini-museum
• Any items needed for displaying artifacts, such as thumbtacks or double-sided tape

1. If your child has an overwhelming number of objects for his museum, try picking a special theme to help winnow it down. It can be as simple as "Tom's Baseball Museum" or as elaborate as "Our Puerto Rican Heritage." Reduce the family pictures and other documents on a photocopier then return the originals to a safe place.

2. Encourage your child to investigate the meaning and origin of the things he collects and make labels with dates and captions for each item. Then have him carefully display his items, grouping objects in a logical way.

3. Your child can make a small catalog to accompany the mini-museum and even send out announcements to family members and friends to come to an exhibit opening.

Millennium Family Portraits

Did you know that in the nineteenth century, a smile was considered too frivolous an expression for a formal portrait? Or that a person shown holding a book in a photograph was a clue, indicating to the viewer that the subject was educated? Every portrait tells a story. You and your family can mark the year 2000 by creating self-portraits, either by taking photographs, by painting, or as outlined here, by drawing—a technique that works well with artistic families.

Materials
• Acid-free heavy-stock paper (at least five sheets per person)
• Acid-free markers

1. Each person should think about how she would like to remembered years from now. What objects would she hold to best reflect her personality? What should the setting be like? Should she place anything in the portrait that reflects her ethnic heritage? What emotion would she like to express?

2. Set up your work area and put out all the supplies, encouraging everyone to try several versions of their self-portraits. When everyone is done, set aside each person's favorite self-portrait.

3. Mark on the back of each portrait the date, the artist, and the place it was drawn. You can even get your self-portraits inexpensively framed.

37

Family Web Album

Now that families are so computer-savvy, they might enjoy creating a scrapbook about their family history on the World Wide Web. Just about anything can go into your private website: recipes, newspaper clippings, songs, proverbs, riddles, jokes, oral histories, drawings, photographs old and new—anything that tells the story of your family. Thanks to a free website service, this process can be very straightforward.

Materials
• A computer with Internet access
• Digital photographs on CD-ROM (ask your film developer for details)

1. MyFamily.com has a free, easy-to-use template for a private family website, including areas for news, chat, photographs, recipe collecting, and more. Parents and children should begin by reviewing the site together (www.myfamily.com), with parents filling out the forms as instructed. There is even a complimentary helpline if you get stumped.

2. Once you know how you want to customize your site, collect the data and images you need, log back in, and set up your site, following the directions. You can then set up your website to notify all your family members to log on and add their own information.

Our Family Cookbook

Perhaps the most common, but overlooked, heirlooms in our families are old family recipes. Special dishes can reveal a lot about our countries of origin, the American regions we have lived in, and the religions we celebrate. You can collect your family's recipes, organize them in a book, then print copies of the cookbook to share with everyone who contributed.

Materials
• Completed recipe forms on white 8 1/2- by 11-inch paper (See Step 1)
• Photographs of family members who created recipes, optional
• Photographs of family members cooking and sharing meals, optional

1. Draw up a list of all the family members from whom you would like to request recipes. Create a form and send several copies to everyone on your list. The form should include blank spaces for filling in the name of the recipe, the name of the contributor, the history of the recipe, the ingredients needed (in order of when they appear in the directions), the cooking directions, and the amount of prep time and cooking time.

2. Explain in an accompanying letter that you plan to copy the recipes into a cookbook, and send a copy to each participant. Give your family deadlines, and follow up with a reminder postcard as the deadline draws near.

3. When your recipes are in, design a cover and an introductory index to all the recipes on the same kind of paper as you used for your form. Lay out the recipes and, if desired, the photographs in the order you like best (from soups to dessert, perhaps, or by cook).

4. Take your layout to your local copy shop and ask them for options, such as glued bindings or spiral bindings. Consider reducing the paper to make a smaller format cookbook. Photographs can be photocopied, too, as well as reduced and enlarged. Request paper samples for both the cover and the inside pages so you can decide what it best for you. Get cost estimates and then ask for as many cookbook copies as you need.

Oral Histories for Kids

Collecting oral histories isn't just for adults. With a little help, kids can use the guidelines on page 36 to gather oral histories. Let children pick a theme or focus for the interview, such as school, holidays, or childhood. And keep in mind a few special considerations.

• Help kids develop questions that link interviewers and narrators, such as: What is your earliest memory? What was your life like when you were my age? What was your favorite book? What do you remember about me when I was younger?

• Have narrators bring photographs, toys, or other family treasures that might interest children.

• Be sensitive to special issues facing adopted children and children whose parents have divorced or remarried.

• Help young interviewers be sensitive to powerful issues that can come up in an interview, such as the difficult experiences some family members may have had. Some parents and narrators will want to avoid these subjects, and others will want to be ready for them. ★

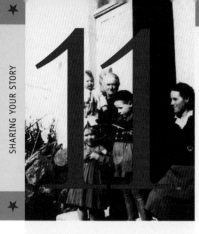

Sharing your story

Add your family
stories via the
My History website:
www.myhistory.org

Your family history connects you to other families and other historians. People tracing their own family histories might discover a lead in yours. A scholar might find anecdotes about your family that will help bring a historical study to life. The critical step is creating an accurate, well-documented family story or history and helping other people locate it.

• Enter your family story or history in a word processing program, print a few copies, and send them on a tour through the family.

• Add your family stories via the **My History** website at www.myhistory.org, or create your own family history website.

• Find out whether your local library or historical society collects family histories and offer to donate yours.

• With other family historians, ask your local library or historical society to begin a collection of local family histories.

• Link your family history website to the appropriate spot in USGenWeb, at www.usgenweb.org ★

Top: **Sal Romano's grandmother Maria Iob and cousins.**
Facing page, top right: **Stefania Iob's class in Cunevo, Italy, 1919.**

The Romanos' story

The first words on Sal Romano's website tell why he started his labor of love. "My introduction to Trentino began with stories told to me as a child—stories about a valley in northern Italy surrounded by mountains, castles, and lakes. These stories fueled a desire to learn more about the area—its people, its culture, its history. A natural progression was to undertake the task of tracing my ancestral ties to Trentino."

Although the stories were of Italy, the storyteller and the audience were both in the United States. The storyteller was Sal's mother, Stefania Iob Romano. The stories she told years ago helped bring forth the family history, Italian history, American history, and hundreds of links to other resources that fill the pages of her son's website at members.aol.com/sromano937.

Years of crop disease, floods, and landslides devastated Trentino in the late 1800s. Thousands of the region's residents, or Trentini, left Italy around the turn of the century. Most headed for South America, but many also began new lives in the mining towns of Colorado, including Maria Banaletti and Roberto Iob, Sal Romano's grandparents. Maria's first husband was killed in a mine explosion and both lost brothers and cousins to mining accidents. Maria and Roberto married in 1907 but remained in the Hastings, Colorado, area only three more years before the hard mining life drove them and their three young children back to Italy. Thousands of mining families followed as the industry

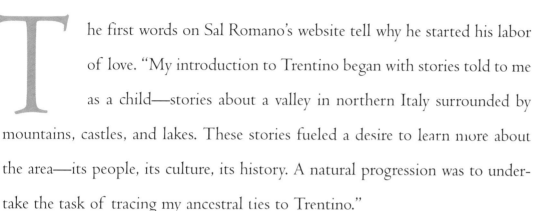

Above: **16th-century arch bearing the Iob family crest.**
Right: **Postcard of West Main Street, Trinidad, Colorado, 1920s**

COMMERCIAL STREET. TRINIDAD. COLO.

declined. The population of Hastings fell from 2,000 in 1909 to 700 in 1912. The waves of immigration they joined were made of countless individual decisions to move—family history pouring into national history. But the history of nations also pushed people toward personal decisions. Stefania's brother

Carlo, an American citizen born in Colorado, left Italy to escape being drafted into Mussolini's army, and later landed on the Normandy beaches as a G.I.

Stefania returned to the United States in 1931 and lived with her sister, Lena. In 1942 she married Salvatore Romano, Sr., and moved to New York City. She taught herself English from comic books, worked in a garment factory, and raised Sal Junior, and his sister. After her husband died in 1957, she supported the family as a seamstress and dressmaker from her home. The family story came full circle when young Salvatore, in the Army himself, visited Trentino in 1967 and decided to explore the region's history and his own, and preserve both.

1900–1909
Nearly two million Italians arrive in the United States, constituting almost one in four immigrants during those years.

1901
Sal Romano's grandmother Maria Banaletti arrives in Colorado mining region.

1902
Maria Banaletti marries Francesco Iob.

1903–04
Members of the Iob and Banaletti families participate in Cripple Creek strike, led by the Western Federation of Miners.

1905
Roberto Iob joins his brother Francesco in Colorado.

1906
Francesco Iob dies in a mining explosion.

1907
Roberto Iob, Sal's grandfather, marries Maria Banaletti.

1907
Economic downturn prompts immigrants to leave the United States in large numbers.

About 1910
Roberto and Maria Iob leave U.S. for Trentino, Italy, with their children including one-year-old Stefania, Sal Romano's mother.

1931
Sal's mother, Stefania Iob, arrives in the United States and lives with her sister. who finds work for Stefania as a seamstress.

1942
Stefania Iob marries Sal Romano, Sr.

1967
On leave from a military tour of duty in Europe, Sal Romano, Jr., visits Trentino, Italy.

12

Connecting with your community

Never underestimate the power of a good story. Some evening, out on the porch, lean over and tell your neighbor about your great aunt the army nurse and let her tell you about her great-grandfather the bootlegger. Look for the connections—your stories and your neighbor's might flow together at some point, probably in a way you don't expect.

Look around the community for more ways to share your family stories. You may find informal conversations where you can simply listen and tell stories. You will at least make a

connection with others and glimpse what it's like to be in their shoes.

You may find more structured programs for collecting or exchanging family stories at your local library, college, or historical society. While you are at it, take the opportunity to check their offerings on state or local history.

Once in awhile, these shared family histories that begin so simply take on a life of their own as documented community histories, exhibits, or heritage trails. Don't concern yourself with that at the start. Just join the conversation.

* You may find family conversations already going at your church, civic club, library, or senior center. If not, why not start one? Invite a historian to join the group to help tie stories together and lend some historical perspective. If you are looking for a historian, ask for a referral from the local college, historical society, or state humanities council.

* Check the local library's schedule of reading and discussion programs. The themes and readings often welcome and inspire the exchange of family stories.

* If you have already begun to gather your family history, find ways to collaborate with others in your community. The more families you include, the more your collected family histories will begin to form a community history. Recruit historians to join the team. The historical society or humanities council may not be able to play a role, but they will be interested to know what you're doing.

* Learn what you can about state and local history from programs offered by historical societies and humanities councils.

* Post one or more stories about your family on the World Wide Web through **www.myhistory.org** and look for other stories there. ★

Communities' stories

Above: **A fruit stand in the French Island archive,**
Left: **Taping oral histories on the island.**
Below: **A postcard photograph of island resident Nelson St. James. He wrote on the back, "How do I look in this uniform?"**

"Let's Talk About It"

At a small library in South Carolina, a discussion of American identity inspired a lively exchange about local families and local history. Based on the book *Lemon Swamp,* the discussion was part of a series developed by the American Library Association (ALA), and funded by the National Endowment for the Humanities. Available across the country, reading and discussion programs connect lifelong learners with books and films. For more information, visit the ALA website at www.ala.org.

An Urban Memoir

Senior residents at Potomac Gardens public housing site in Washington, D.C., met with public historians for two years to assemble their stories and review their photographs and favorite objects. The historians learned about migration from the rural south to Washington, D.C., and everyday life in the city since the 1920s. Grants from the Humanities Council of Washington, D.C., helped produce an oral history project, "In Search of Common Ground," a documentary video, and an exhibition at the Anacostia Museum.

A French-Speaking Place

On French Island, Maine, a small group of residents started asking their neighbors to talk about life there when they were young—simply to capture some of the history of this French-speaking community before it disappeared. With the help of many people in the community and a grant from the Maine Humanities Council, their oral histories evolved into a photo-graphic archive, a website, and an illustrated history of the community. To see how a small family history project can grow, visit www.old-town.lib.me.us/nos/default.htm.

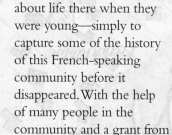

Two of the participants in the program "In Search of Common Ground: Senior Citizens and Community Life at Potomac Gardens."

13 Finding help

Help a local history organization set up a "Family History Day."

★ Look for case studies of community oral history projects at **www.myhistory.org**

Below: **Participants in The Century Project, young and old, gather in the Hall of Flags at the Maine Statehouse.**

Preserving family and community history is part of the mission of local libraries, historical societies, museums, humanities councils, colleges, and universities—and you can help. Volunteers are crucial to local history projects, so get in touch with organizations like these and sign up.

• Volunteer for local oral history projects. Historical organizations aren't the only sponsors: senior centers, fraternal organizations, and professional associations sometimes collect oral histories. The skills you've developed in gathering your own family history will be useful, and transcribing oral histories is also vital work. Transcripts are still one of the best means of storing and sharing oral histories.

• Help a local history organization set up a "Family History Day." People from the community can bring in photographs, diaries, naturalization papers, and other family treasures to learn a little more about them from the staff of the museum or historical association. The local organizations get a better idea of what is out there in the community and can photocopy documents and photographs that might be important for programs or collections. ★

Making the story grow

Harbor West Sound, Wash. Orcas Island.
Hall Photo. No 1

T.W. Ransom

An Island in Washington State

The Orcas Island Oral History Project has a forty-year history, and students and volunteers have been crucial to the project throughout its life. In the 1950s, a University of Washington student began an oral history project with residents of island, off the Washington coast near Bellingham. Other local residents and scholars picked up threads of the project and added photographs of some residents in the 1970s. In the 1980s, teachers on the island assigned students to interview their elders, and these recordings joined the growing oral history collection. In 1999—through the work of professional historians, photographers, storytellers, performers, and volunteers—the project culminated in an exhibition and series of public programs. Both celebrate the island's past and share with its residents the permanent archive of local history gathered and preserved over the years.

Counterclockwise, from top:
One of the six adjoining homestead cabins that are part of the Orcas Island Historical Museum.

West Sound, Orcas Island, Washington, about 1890.

The late Alfred O'Neill, subject of an oral history.

Main Street in East Sound, Orcas Island, about 1939.

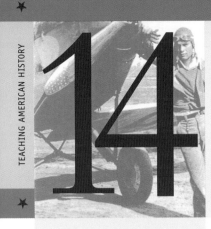

14 Teaching American history through family history

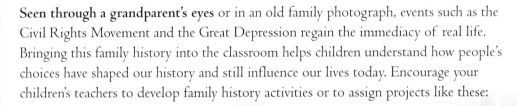

Encourage your children's teachers to develop family history projects.

Seen through a grandparent's eyes or in an old family photograph, events such as the Civil Rights Movement and the Great Depression regain the immediacy of real life. Bringing this family history into the classroom helps children understand how people's choices have shaped our history and still influence our lives today. Encourage your children's teachers to develop family history activities or to assign projects like these:

Preschool
Class Family Quilt—Give each child a square of construction paper to decorate in class and at home with emblems of his or her family life: pictures of family members (including pets), mementos of family pastimes and travels, words and images that evoke the family heritage. Form a quilt with the finished squares on a bulletin board. Have each child talk about his or her square, then talk as a group about the things their families share.

Elementary School
Where I'm From—Combine geography with family history by having students research the regions and countries that are part of their heritage. As a class, create a large world map on which each student can plot his or her family's travels over time. Discuss the range of countries and cultures represented, the distances covered over many lifetimes, and where the paths of students' families may have crossed.

MAMIE
FOR
FIRST LADY

Middle School

The Impact of Events—Use family history to help students understand the impact of landmark events. For events still in living memory, such as World War II, the space race, or the movement of women into the workplace, students can interview family members to learn how an event affected their lives—or why it didn't. For events long past, such as the California Gold Rush or the Dawes Act, students can research family documents or family traditions to create timelines that show how these events changed their families' lives.

High School

"Auto-biography"—Today, most American's lives are shaped in part by "auto-mobility"— the freedom to live far from the workplace, visit distant relatives, even drive to the wilderness. Have students create family auto-biographies, which might include pictures of cars their ancestors have owned, oral histories of memorable roadtrips, and a comparison of the automobile's influence on family life across several generations.

A Note for Teachers

At **www.myhistory.org**, you can find lesson plans and classroom-ready resources in family history for all grade levels. Look here for lessons that integrate learning across the curriculum—in literature, language arts, geography, social studies, civics, technology, art, music, and other disciplines. In addition, there are many activities and projects adaptable for learning outside the classroom, in community centers, by youth groups, and within the home.

Plot the migrations of your ancestors on a world and U.S. map.

★ Visit "Teaching with My History" at **www.myhistory.org**

Keep in mind that family history can touch on sensitive and sometimes painful issues, such as the difficult experiences some family members may have had. Teachers should try to anticipate concerns such as these and respect the privacy of students and their families. ★

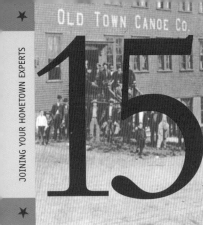

15

Joining your hometown experts

After you visit, you may want to volunteer.

Visit your local historical society and public library—find out what's already there. All local historical organizations depend in part on the good will of the community, so you may want to volunteer. You might live near a state or regional historical organization, and those places often need volunteer help, too. Check the list of organizations in this book for possibilities. Local historical societies are particularly interested in acquiring documented family items. ★

©Chinese Historical Society of America

Fong Soo Foon's story

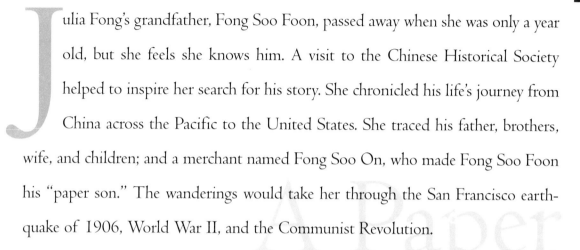

MY HISTORY IS AMERICA'S HISTORY

Julia Fong's grandfather, Fong Soo Foon, passed away when she was only a year old, but she feels she knows him. A visit to the Chinese Historical Society helped to inspire her search for his story. She chronicled his life's journey from China across the Pacific to the United States. She traced his father, brothers, wife, and children; and a merchant named Fong Soo On, who made Fong Soo Foon his "paper son." The wanderings would take her through the San Francisco earthquake of 1906, World War II, and the Communist Revolution.

Fong Soo Foon was born in Taishan, China, in 1902, into a family and a village struggling against poverty. Even as a young man, he knew he could never be a farmer nor stay in Taishan. Hope for a better life in the United States drew him, as it had thousands of Chinese since the Gold Rush days of the 1840s.

Fong Soo Foon's father forbade him to leave. Two of his brothers had already immigrated to the United States and were plagued by debts. The United States didn't want him. The Chinese Exclusion Act of 1882 prohibited immigration by all Chinese except scholars, diplomats, and certain merchants and barred any Chinese from becoming naturalized citizens. Merely a laborer, Fong Soo Foon knew that his only chance to bypass this law and reach America was to buy someone else's identity for a huge sum and convince immigration officials that he was the son of a legal Chinese resident of the United States.

"Paper sons," in a way, were children of the San Francisco Earthquake of 1906. It destroyed birth certificates and citizenship papers for many of the naturalized citizens and legal Chinese immigrants in California, who could then claim they had left behind sons or daughters in their homeland. Young men and women in China paid thousands of dollars to assume these identities and come to the United States.

Top: **Fong Soo Foon, Julia Fong's grandfather.**
Above: **Jimmy Fong, left, with his mother, Yee Fee King, and sister Dorsee.**
Left: **The U.S. Quarantine Station at Angel Island, California.** ©Chinese Historical Society of America.

Fong Soo Foon

1848–49

Gold discovered in California and Gold Rush begins.

1860

35,000 Chinese are living in California, one out of ten residents of the state.

1882

The Chinese Exclusion Act suspends immigration from China for 10 years; it is extended indefinitely in 1904.

1902

Julia Fong's grandfather Fong Soo Foon born in Taishan, China, the fifth son in a family of 11 children.

1906

San Francisco Earthquake destroys immigrant records, opening the door to "paper sons" from China.

1910

Angel Island opens as an immigrant station and begins processing applications.

1921

Fong leaves China for the United States. After interrogation, he receives a Certificate of Identity.

Above: **Jimmy Fong,** third from left, back row, stayed with his relatives in Hong Kong for eight years while he waited to join his family in the U.S. Left: A transcript of Fong Soo Foon's immigration interview at Angel Island, 1921.

Fong Soo Foon eventually won his father's blessing. With help from his brother, he borrowed $3,000 to become the paper son of Fong Soo On, a merchant in Sacramento. He studied the details of his new identity for months and finally boarded the S.S. *Nanking* for the United States. He reached San Francisco on October 14, 1921, and on November 3, began his cycle of interviews at the Angel Island Immigration Station in San Francisco Bay, the "Ellis Island of the West."

Immigration officials interviewed Fong Soo Foon three times, asking questions such as where did you live? When did your family move there? Which house? How many entrance doors to the house? Do the houses in your row touch? Where was the well? What material was the schoolhouse made of? They also interviewed the merchant Fong Soo On and other witnesses, asked the same questions, and compared the answers. One immigration official found contradictions in the testimony and recommended that Fong Soo Foon be denied admission to the United States.

A week later a second inspector read the interviews differently, overturned the original decision, and transformed the lives of Fong Soo Foon and his family. On December 24, he passed through the immigration station, deep in debt, alone, without work, and carrying his new American Certificate of Identity.

Fong Soo Foon found work in a laundry, one of the few jobs available to Chinese immigrants in the United States. He worked hard, paid off his debts in just a few years, and began to send money home. However, he seldom left the safety of Chinatown—a haven from a society that distrusted Chinese.

In his new country, Fong Soo Foon still felt deep ties to China. He saved money for a trip back, but turned 21 in the meantime. His age invalidated his original papers, so he added a new layer to his identity. He presented himself to immigration officials as a part owner of the Jin Fook Company, which sold dry goods, groceries, and general merchandise in San Francisco. He memorized his facts well, and by the end of 1924, Fong Soo

Foon was a paper son and a paper business partner, on his way to China.

Fong Soo Foon's trip back to his homeland began a cycle of reunion, marriage, parenthood, immigration, and separation that lasted 34 years, until 1958. He married Yee Fee King when he first returned to China. But she could not bear to leave her family and homeland, so he returned to the United States alone. He sent money to her faithfully, saved for other trips to China, and returned there in 1932 and 1939. On his last trip he fled the country just ahead of invading Japanese troops and the outbreak of World War II.

Fong Soo Foon and Yee Fee King had two daughters and a son—Bik To, Dorsee, and Jimmy. Bik To married a Chinese veteran of the U.S. military and immigrated to the United States in 1945. After the Chinese Exclusion Act was lifted in 1943,

1924

Immigration Act establishes quotas for each nationality—2 percent of their representation in 1890 census.

Working as a laundry man, Fong earns enough to pay off his debts. He becomes a "paper business partner" with San Francisco grocers to obtain a new visa and buys passage to China.

1925

While in China, Fong marries Yee Fee King. She wants to stay in her homeland, and gives birth to their first daughter in 1926.

1932

Fong returns to China for another visit; second daughter born in 1933.

1939

Fong visits China for the last time and cuts visit short due to the outbreak of the Sino-Japanese War; third child, Jimmy, who is Julia's father, born in 1940.

1943

Chinese Exclusion Act repealed.

1945

Fong's daughter Bik To marries a Chinese veteran of World War II and immigrates into the United States.

1949

Fong becomes a U.S. citizen; Yee Fee King comes to the United States and leaves two younger children—Dorsee and Jimmy—in the care of relatives in China.

Top right: **Prospecting for gold near Nevada City, California, 1852.**
Above right: **Restaurant and Tea Garden, Chinatown, San Francisco.** ©Chinese Historical Society of America.

Left: **From left to right, Fong Soo Foon, Yee Fee King, their daughters Dorsee and Bik To, and her husband and children.**
Below: **Jimmy Fong.**
Bottom: **Julia Fong and her maternal great-grandmother, in China.**

1951

Dorsee and Jimmy escape Communist Revolution and stay with cousins in Hong Kong; Dorsee becomes a "paper daughter" and joins her family in the United States.

1958

After many attempts, Fong's petition to bring his son to America is approved, and Jimmy joins his family in the United States.

1958

Angel Island becomes a national park.

Fong Soo Foon began the process of becoming an American citizen, but the small quota for naturalized Chinese kept him waiting six years. In 1949, Yee Fee King was granted a visa to join her husband, and Fong Soo Foon found a chance to bring Jimmy over as a paper son. Jimmy's opportunity fell through as Yee Fee King's visa was about to expire, and she faced the same kind of terrible choice that once confronted her husband. She could either give up her chance to immigrate, or leave behind her two youngest children, now sixteen and nine. Not knowing if she would ever have another chance to join her husband, Yee Fee King left her children with her mother and sailed from China in 1950, filled with determination to bring her children to the United States.

Poverty kept Dorsee and Jimmy trapped at their village. The villagers, desperate for money, refused to allow the children to leave because they believed that Fong Soo Foon would send them more money. The next year, Dorsee devised a scheme to travel with her brother to Hong Kong, supposedly to retrieve more money from her father and bring it back to the village. Once there, she and Jimmy found distant relatives to stay with. Shortly afterward, Dorsee had the chance to become a "paper daughter" herself, but only if she

left within four months. On September 11, Dorsee sadly told her little brother to be a good boy and do well in school before she stepped on a plane for the United States, one day before her papers expired.

Jimmy was now 10 years old and the only member of his family left behind. Jimmy's parents sent him many letters and as much money as they could, and repeatedly petitioned the U.S. government to grant him a visa. Out of frustration and loneliness, Jimmy took up calligraphy and poured his emotions into the intricate, elegant Chinese characters. In 1958—seven years after his sister left Hong Kong and nine years after his father became a naturalized citizen—Jimmy was finally granted permission to join his family in America and meet his father for the first time.

SOME FORTY YEARS LATER, JIMMY'S DAUGHTER JULIA took her fourth grade class to the Chinese Historical Society in San Francisco and noticed a program called "In Search of Roots." The discovery of the program matched her budding interest in her heritage. As an intern she interviewed her father, aunts, and other relatives, pored over immigration files, returned to China, and toured the Angel Island Immigration Center. She then reconstructed the story of her grandfather's refusal to let poverty, distance, or immigration laws keep him from his dream or his family. And she transformed her own indifference and even embarrassment over her family's struggle to a source of intense pride.

SAVING YOUR FAMILY TREASURES

MY HISTORY IS AMERICA'S HISTORY

Simple steps for preserving
your family heirlooms and
combating the perils of rubber
bands, adhesives, acidic paper,
heat, light, and humidity

Family treasures link generations in a deep, personal way. Anyone who has seen a great-grandmother's doll, an uncle's baseball cap, or a photo of a relative going off to war knows how moving these pieces of history can be. These guidelines will help you take care of your family treasures.

Not everyone will be able to follow every piece of advice, but do what you can. Even simple, inexpensive steps can go a long way toward preserving your heirlooms.

And you should keep in mind that enjoying family heirlooms and preserving them is always a balancing act. For fragile objects like crystal or heirloom clothing, the tradeoffs are easy to see—the more you handle them the greater the risk. But exposing almost any family treasure to everyday changes in light, heat, and humidity will eventually cause damage. The advice here will help you decide where to draw the line.

By taking care of your family's precious objects, you give three gifts: the treasures themselves, your dedication in preserving them, and a richer understanding of your family's history.

Preserving Your Past

All objects deteriorate over time, so start caring for them now. Make sure to identify, photograph, and maintain records of your treasures. Describe the history and condition of each object; note who made, purchased, or used it; and tell what it means to your family. Always identify individuals in a family photograph and the time and place it was taken. Getting the details down on paper is rewarding in itself, gives you a way to monitor the condition of your treasures. Your family treasures can also suggest how your family history fits into the larger story of the nation's past.

"Consult a Conservator"

These three words of advice appear often in these guidelines. Sometimes there's no substitute for expert help. Professional conservators understand what causes the deterioration of many different materials, and how to slow or prevent it. They master their subject through years of apprenticeship, university programs, or both, and usually have a specialty, such as paintings or books. A local museum, library, or historical society may know where to find conservators in your area and can offer other advice on preserving your treasures.

SIMPLE STEPS TO PRESERVING YOUR TREASURES

Light, temperature, humidity, pollutants, pests, and handling all affect how rapidly objects decay. Here are a few basic things you can do to save your heirlooms:

- **Display or store your treasures in a stable, clean environment.** Filtered air, a temperature of 72° F or below, and humidity between 45 and 55 percent are ideal goals. Day to day, try to avoid dampness, too much heat, and dramatic changes in temperature and humidity. If you feel comfortable, your treasures probably will, too.

- **Location, location, location!** Display and store your treasures away from heat sources, outside walls, basements, and attics. Don't hang Great Grandpa's portrait over the radiator or fireplace.

- **Shun the sun and fluorescent light.** They fade and discolor most treasures and are especially dangerous to fabrics and anything on paper.

- **Check for signs of pests.** Holes in furniture or textiles, wood shavings, and tiny droppings are all evidence. Consult a conservator if you spot trouble.

- **Heirloom allergies.** Historic objects can be harmed by abrasive cleaners; dry-cleaner's bags; glues, adhesive tapes, and labels; pins and paper clips; acidic wood, cardboard, or paper; and pens and markers.

- **Even if it is broken, don't fix it!** A smudged painting, torn photograph, or broken vase may seem easy to fix. They aren't. Well-intended but amateur repairs usually do more harm than good. Consult a conservator for advice on valued items.

The next twelve pages give advice on display, handling, storage, and basic care for the most typical family treasures.

GOOD CHEMISTRY

Acid is found naturally in many kinds of paper and wood. It is acid that makes newspapers yellow and brittle so quickly. Throughout these guidelines, you will see references to *acid-free* products and certain plastics. These materials are recommended for display and storage because they will not harm your family treasures.

Here are a few other terms you will encounter in this guide and in supply catalogs:

Buffered and Unbuffered: All materials are either acidic, neutral, or alkaline. Acidic materials will slowly destroy your heirlooms. Acid-free materials may be buffered (slightly alkaline) to help counteract the effects of acids or unbuffered (neutral). Buffered materials are safe for most treasures but choose unbuffered for blueprints, photographs, and fabrics.

Plastics and Foams: Several kinds of plastics are useful in preserving your treasures. Polyethylene, polypropylene, polyester, polycarbonate, and acrylic products are all stable materials that can help protect your heirlooms.

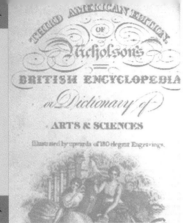

books

PRESERVATION TIP GUIDELINES

Keep treasured books out of attics and basements.

Use and Display

To remove a book from the shelf, push back the books on either side and grasp it along the spine; don't pull the top of the book with your finger.

Open books carefully, and don't press down on the pages to flatten the spine.

Stand books upright on shelves. Support them with books or bookends of similar size. Display very large books flat.

Storage

Store books on shelves lined with polyester film or heavy, acid-free paperboard. Avoid direct contact with wooden shelves.

Protect damaged books by storing them in acid-free boxes and inspect them regularly. If you see signs of mold or pests, contact a conservation professional.

Care

Dust books at least once a year with a magnetic dust cloth or a vacuum on very low suction using the brush attachment covered with cheesecloth.

Don't use oils, leather dressings, saddle soap, polish, or adhesive tape on books.

ceramics, glass, and stone

Use

Handle your objects one at a time with clean, dry hands. Use two hands to lift each one.

Avoid using special pieces to store food or hold live flower arrangements; don't fill ceramics or glass with colored water.

Display and Storage

Display and store ceramics and glass away from direct sunlight on level shelves. Do not expose them to extreme temperatures.

Keep pieces separate. Use flannel cloth, paper towels, or thin polyethylene foam to layer stacked plates or to wrap individual items for packing.

Care

Dust glass, ceramic, or stone objects with a magnetic dust cloth. Do not use dusting sprays, polishes, or commercial cleaners.

Hand wash porcelain, stoneware, and other glazed ceramics and glass in warm water and a little dishwashing liquid. Dry with a soft towel. Never clean them in an automatic dishwasher.

Do not wash *unglazed* ceramics and glass or ceramics with gold edging, hand-painted decorations, or repairs. Dust with a soft-bristled brush or vacuum with a brush attachment.

Bring outdoor stone sculpture inside during cold weather or cover with burlap.

If a treasured object breaks, wrap all the pieces in paper towels or tissue paper and contact a conservator.

PRESERVATION TIP GUIDELINES

Using any ceramic or glass object places it at risk. Save special, valuable, or damaged pieces for display only.

fabrics

Use and Display

Wearing heirloom clothing always introduces the risk of rips or stains. If you must wear it, avoid antiperspirants and makeup.

Wear cotton gloves to handle heirloom fabrics. Move the fabrics on a support or in their boxes.

Display fabrics flat or hung at an angle to reduce pull. When you bring your textiles out into the light, keep the light low and the occasion brief.

Support clothing or costumes with a plastic hanger padded with clean white cotton cloth to the the same size and shape as the article's shoulders.

Storage

Store folded textiles in acid-free boxes with acid-free tissue between layers, or wrap them in clean white sheets. Pad the folds with tissue to avoid creasing.

To store rugs or heavy blankets, roll them with the pile outward and wrap with washed muslin (undyed 100 percent cotton).

Care

Never wash or dry clean antique fabrics. Blot any spills immediately and seek expert advice.

Sturdy items can be cleaned with a vacuum cleaner on low suction, using the brush attachment covered with cheesecloth.

Keep pests out by practicing good housekeeping. If you suspect problems, consult a conservator—don't use pesticides or mothballs without professional guidance.

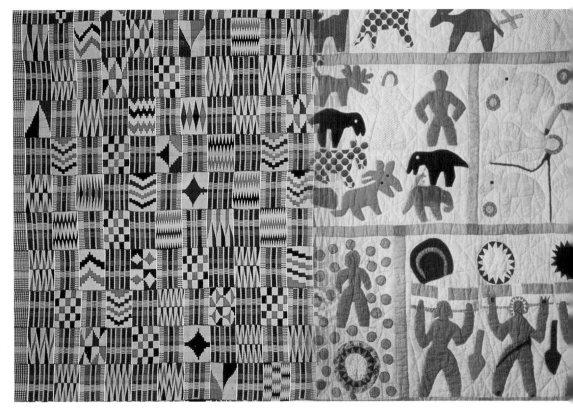

precious paper

Use and Display

Do not laminate special papers; the process can be harmful, and it is irreversible. Consult a conservator before using any commercial deacidification products.

Avoid folding and unfolding papers; it weakens them. Place oversized items flat on larger pieces of acid-free matboard (and see page 67, "Matting, Mounting, and Framing").

Storage

Store paper materials in darkness and ration their time in the light—especially their moments in the sun.

Store loose papers unfolded in acid-free paper or polyester folders. Put fragile or torn documents in individual folders and keep the folders in acid-free (not wooden) boxes.

Highly acidic materials like newspaper clippings often become yellow and brittle quickly. Separate them from other papers and photocopy the clippings onto acid-free paper.

Bugs love glue and paper. Keep an eye out for creatures feasting on your precious papers.

Care

Never use paper clips, staples, rubber bands, tape, or glue on important papers.

Consult a conservator if you find evidence of dirt or mold on prized papers.

★ **PLAN AHEAD. If you are creating a family tree or an oral history, use safe, durable acid-free materials.**

PRESERVATION TIP GUIDELINES

Don't underestimate the power of nature. Acidity, light, and high temperature and humidity are the greatest threats to your family papers.

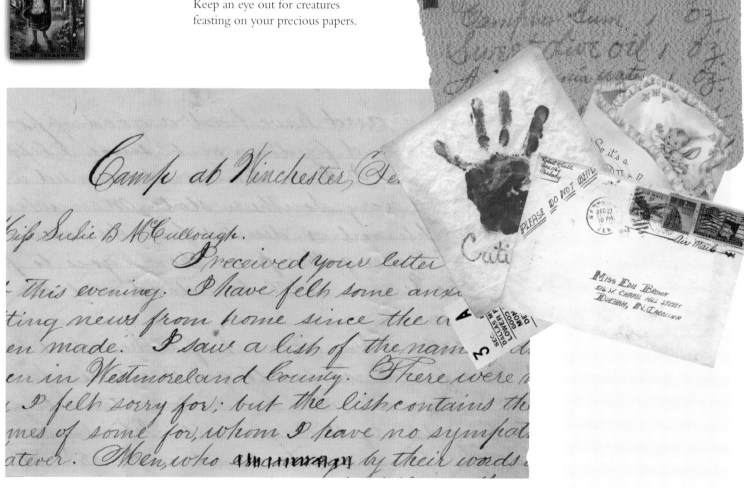

furniture

**The key to preserving
furniture:
"Handle with Care."**

Use and Display

Display furniture in the lowest possible light. Keep it out of sunlight and avoid shining lamps directly onto important pieces.

Use felt or another soft cloth to pad the base of any object placed on furniture. Coasters will help protect surfaces from food, water, alcohol, candle wax, and scratches.

Avoid using or moving damaged furniture.

Move furniture slowly and grip it firmly with both hands below the center of gravity. Don't drag furniture along the floor, and use dollies for heavy pieces.

Storage

Keep historic furniture out of attics and basements. Check regularly for evidence of insects and mold.

Care

Don't use commercial oils that claim to "feed" the finish or sprays containing silicone. If necessary, clean wooden surfaces with a lint-free cloth lightly dampened with a mild soap-and-water solution.

Use paste wax sparingly, once a year, to make light dusting easier. Wax around, not on, damaged areas.

Clean upholstery by vacuuming carefully through a plastic screen, and avoid stain-resistant treatments.

Wipe up any spills immediately. If a stain remains or you see signs of damage, contact a conservator.

Original finishes and upholstery are very important to the value of heirloom furniture. Do not alter or remove them if possible.

paintings

Use and Display

Display your paintings away from sources of heat, humidity, pollution, and sunlight. An interior wall, out of direct sunlight, is the safest place to hang a painting.

Illuminate paintings with cool fiber-optic picture lights. Avoid incandescent bulbs and track lighting, which can heat the surface.

Attach cardboard backing to paintings. Hang by the frame whenever possible and use mirror plate hangers or D-rings instead of eye hooks.

Hang paintings securely from two mounting points, securing mirror hangers to the frame.

Use picture or mirror hangers on the walls—not nails or self-adhesive hooks.

Handling or moving paintings always puts them at risk. Carry paintings with both hands and ask for help with larger pictures.

Storage

To store a painting, trim pieces of cardboard to match the frame and place them over the front and back of the painting. Wrap the painting in paper and keep it upright away from foot traffic. Do not store paintings in basements or attics.

Care

Dust oil paintings very gently with a clean and soft brush (an art supply store is a good source). Work from the top down. Use the brush for this chore only and store it in a clean bag. Never use sprays, waxes, polishes, or oils.

Improper cleaning or restoration techniques can destroy valuable paintings. Have them cleaned and repaired by a professional.

PRESERVATION TIP GUIDELINES

The greatest threats to paintings are careless handling and rapid changes in temperature and humidity.

Works of Art on Paper

There are more works of art on paper than on canvas—sketches, watercolors, drawings, and posters, for example. Care for them as you would other paper treasures: limit exposure to extremes of light and temperature; use acid-free materials for display and storage. Handle some with special care: "powdery" art such as pastels or charcoal drawings will smudge easily and fingerprints can stain glossy posters.

Frame them correctly or store them in protective matting or folders.

photographs and slides

Display

Display copies of photographs whenever possible and store the originals separately. Always make copies of damaged photos.

Protect photographic prints behind glass or acrylic that filters ultraviolet light, such as appropriate kinds of plexiglass.

Frame photographic prints with acid-free stable materials. Use ragboard mats that pass the photographic activity test (PAT). The mats should be unbuffered for color photos and buffered for black and white.

Use acid-free—not magnetic or self-adhesive—photo albums. Protect color transparencies, slides, and negatives in stable plastic pages.

Storage

Store photos and negatives in envelopes or folders made of stable plastic film or acid-free paper. Place the envelopes in acid-free boxes and don't pack them too tightly.

Avoid storing photos in contact with kraft paper, glassine envelopes, mounting board with high wood-pulp content, rubber cement, or glue.

Care

Handle photographs, negatives, and slides only by the edges and avoid touching the image. Wearing cotton gloves is a good idea.

Try to label photographs on the backs of frames or on album or storage pages. If necessary, use a soft, No. 2 pencil to write lightly on the back.

Keep photos and negatives out of the reach of pests.

scrapbooks and albums

Display and Storage

Shelve small and medium–sized scrapbooks and albums upright. If they are large, bulge open, or contain loose items, display or store them flat.

If a scrapbook's cover is loose, tie the book closed with linen or cotton tape.

If individual items are loose or a scrapbook is damaged, store it in an acid-free box or wrap it in acid-free paper.

Care

News clippings and other yellowed papers are highly acidic and may harm items on nearby pages. If you can safely remove these clippings from a scrapbook, photocopy them onto acid-free paper, put the copies in the book, and save the originals separately if they have handwritten information.

If you can't remove acidic materials like news clippings from a scrapbook, separate them from other items with sheets of acid-free paper or polyester film.

Use only plastic or acid-free paper corners to reattach loose items. For all other repairs, seek professional advice.

Tips on making a new family album:

- Select safe materials such as acid-free binders, pages, and paper corners and stable plastics for sleeves, pocket pages, and stamp mounts.

- Photocopy newspaper clippings onto acid-free paper and consult a conservator about the stability of other photographs and papers.

- Cutting original photographs or other family heirlooms into decorative shapes diminishes their value; use copies.

PRESERVATION TIP GUIDELINES

Handle old scrapbooks and albums with care. Never repair them with tape or glue.

silver and other metals

Silver

Use

Oils in the skin will etch the surface of silver. Use a soft cotton cloth to buff off fingerprints or wear gloves for frequent handling.

Storage

Store silver at moderate temperature and low humidity—away from corrosive agents like salt, sugar, acidic foods, paper, wool, rubber (including rubber bands), unsealed wood, or plastic.

Cloth specially treated for protecting silver is available in bags and rolls for wrapping individual pieces for storage. You can also wrap pieces in sulfur- and acid-free tissue paper and seal them in a bag with a commercial antitarnish strip.

Care

Avoid commercial polishes and dips containing dilute sulfuric acid.

To polish silver, use a paste made of calcium carbonate and a mild detergent solution, applied with cotton balls. Rinse with water to remove residues and dry with a soft, lint-free cloth.

Treat all-silver jewelry like silver objects, but never immerse jewelry with gems and semi-precious materials in water.

Other precious metals

Polishing can destroy the look of metallic coatings, such as gold-plate, silver-gilt, golden varnishes, and ormolu (an alloy of copper and tin or zinc that looks like gold).

Bronze, brass, copper, and gold-plated metals may have an original patina or a factory-applied lacquer. Clean gently with a damp cloth.Bright, unlacquered brass and copper can be cleaned like silver.

Pewter and nickel silver (also known as German silver) should be dusted, only occasionally washed, and then thoroughly dried.

leather and other organic materials

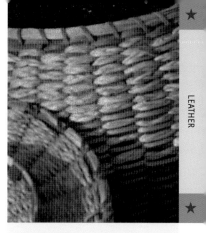

Use and Display

Baskets, leather, and other organic objects are among the most vulnerable family heirlooms. Handling them frequently can shorten their lifespans.

Never nail, tack, or tape objects to the wall or hang them by their own straps or handles.

Secure objects on display with interior and exterior supports that are padded with acid-free materials.

Storage

Use acid-free boxes and polyethylene foam for packing and storing. To prevent distortion, gently pad the shape of the object with acid-free tissue paper.

Care

Lift organic materials below the center of gravity. Don't pick them up by their edges, rims, straps, or handles.

Use a tray or box to carry articles that are fragile, supple, or have dangling parts.

Clean undecorated and unpainted baskets, mats, leather, fur, and wooden objects with a low-powered vacuum cleaner, using the brush attachment covered with cheesecloth. Never apply water or cleaning agents.

Never apply waxes, oils, leather dressings, or other coatings to objects made of organic materials.

PRESERVATION TIP GUIDELINES

Objects made from plants and animals are always at risk from insects, light, and changes in humidity. Keep them in stable, protected environments and inspect them regularly.

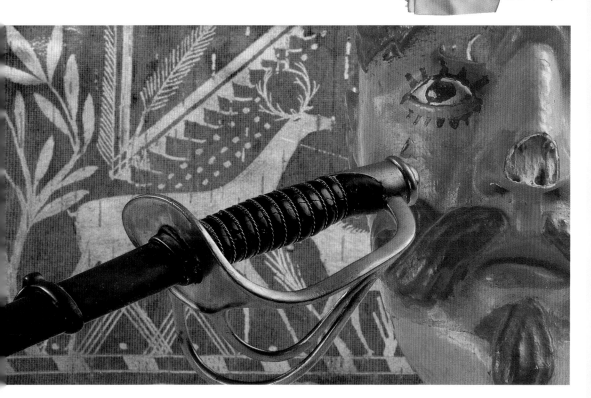

videotapes and audiotapes

The images and sounds captured on videotapes and audiotapes do not last. Take tapes in poor condition or obsolete formats to experts equipped to reformat or copy them.

Use

Handle only the cassettes, never the tape surfaces.

Buy good quality audio- and videotapes—they're thicker and stronger. Record videotapes at standard speed (SP rather than EP) for better images. Break off the tab on a video-cassette to prevent accidentally recording over important moments.

Insert and eject tapes at blank points, and pause them as little as possible. When you're done, rewind the tape and remove it from the tape player right away.

Avoid playing valuable tapes on unfamiliar or suspect equipment.

Storage

Keep tapes away from sources of magnetic fields—electric lines, fluorescent lights, electric motors, and magnets.

Store reels and cassettes on end, like books, in labeled, hard-plastic containers. Keep them in cool, dry areas, away from dust and direct sunlight.

Care

Make extra copies of valuable tapes and store them in a safe deposit box, or with a friend or relative.

Read the manuals for your audiocassette player and VCR to learn about proper operation and routine maintenance. Clean the recording heads on schedule and use dust covers on your equipment.

matting, mounting, and framing

A frame may be important in own right. Consult an expert before replacing or repairing it.

Dust frames with a magnetic cloth or a soft brush and do not decorate them with holiday greenery or ornaments.

Always identify the item you are mounting or framing. Any paper-based treasure can be labeled on the back along the edge with a soft No. 2 pencil. Write gently.

Use only acid-free matting and backing boards.

Select safe materials to attach the paper to the backing board; acid-free photo corners; tissue-paper hinges applied with wheat starch paste; or gummed acid-free paper.

Never use spray mount, rubber cement or other glue, adhesive tape or pressure-sensitive backing.

Cover the image with acrylic sheets or glass to filter out ultraviolet light. Use only glass for artworks in powdery media like chalk, charcoal, or pastels.

Don't let photographs, paper treasures, prints, paintings, or drawings touch glass that covers them. Use a window mat to separate the work from the acrylic or glass.

Fabrics can be mounted onto a support made by covering an acid-free board or stretcher with washed 100 percent cotton. Sew the fabric onto the cloth by hand. You can identify the heirloom with a hand-stitched label made from cotton tape.

★ If you don't want to frame papers or photographs yourself, take these guidelines to a framing store.

PRESERVATION TIP GUIDELINES

Framing or mounting a precious heirloom with the wrong materials can do more harm than good. Acidic matboard, brown backing paper, and cardboard will speed the decay of prints, fabrics, and photographs.

For more information

The resources below offer more detailed advice about preserving your family treasures. Some of the information is intended for specialists or professionals, but the sites also have useful advice for beginners.

The American Institute for Conservation of Historic and Artistic Works (AIC) provides a free guide service to help locate conservation professionals and publishes a series of free pamphlets on conservation topics. Information is available at the AIC website, aic.stanford.edu, or contact:

1717 K Street, NW, Suite 200
Washington, DC 20006
(202) 452-9545
(202) 452-9328 fax

Heritage Preservation
publishes *Caring for Your Collections*, an informative fully illustrated guide to conservation and preventive maintenance for individual collectors. For more information visit the Heritage Preservation website at www.heritagepreservation.org or contact:

1730 K Street, NW, Suite 566
Washington, DC 20006
(202) 634-1422
(202) 634-1435 fax

Smithsonian Institution Press
sells *Conservation Concerns: A Guide for Collectors and Curators*, published by the Cooper-Hewitt National Museum of Design, Smithsonian Institution. For information, call (800) 782-4612.

Pages 54-68 from the Concise Preservation Text, © 1999 by Heritage Preservation

Regional Document Centers

Amigos Library Services, Inc.
14400 Midway Road
Dallas, TX 75244-3509
800-843-8482 or 972-851-8000
www.amigos.org

Balboa Art Conservation Center
PO Box 3755
San Diego, CA 92163-1755
619-236-9702

Conservation Center for Art and Historic Artifacts
264 South 23rd Street
Philadelphia, PA 19103
215-545-0613
www.ccaha.org

Gerald R. Ford Conservation Center
1326 South 32nd Street
Omaha, NE 68105
402-595-1180
www.nebraskahistory.org

Harpers Ferry Center
Division of Conservation
National Park Service
PO Box 50
Harpers Ferry, WV 25425-0050
304-535-6228 or 304/535-6139
www.nps.gov/hfc/conservation

Intermuseum Conservation Association
Allen Art Building
Oberlin, OH 44074
440-775-7331
www.oberlin.edu/~ica

Northeast Document Conservation Center
100 Brickstone Square, 4th Floor
Andover, MA 01810-1494
978-470-1010
www.nedcc.org

Peebles Island Resource Center
Bureau of Historic Sites
New York State Office of Parks, Recreation & Historic Preservation
PO Box 219
Peebles Island
Waterford, NY 12188
518-237-8643 ext. 225 or 226

Rocky Mountain Conservation Center
University of Denver
2420 South University Blvd.
Denver, CO 80208
303-733-2712
www.du.edu/rmcc

The Southeastern Library Network Preservation Services
1438 W. Peachtree St., NW, Suite 200
Atlanta, GA 30309-2955
800-999-8558 and 404-892-0943
www.solinet.net/

Straus Center for Conservation
Harvard University Art Museums
32 Quincy Street
Cambridge, MA 02138
617-495-2392
www.artmuseums.harvard.edu

Textile Conservation Center
American Textile History Museum
491 Dutton Street
Lowell, MA 01854
978-441-1198

Textile Conservation Workshop
3 Main Street
South Salem, NY 10590
914-763-5805

Upper Midwest Conservation Association
2400 Third Avenue South
Minneapolis, MN 55404
612-870-3120
www.preserveart.org

Williamstown Art Conservation Center
225 South Street
Williamstown, MA 01267
413-458-5741

RESOURCE GUIDE

The succeeding pages can help you get started in exploring your family's history and the history of the United States. The lists here include information about books, films, historical societies, and places to visit. They are just a sampling of what is available. More resources can be found at **www.myhistory.org.**

Many of the organizations listed in this guide provide online information about their collections, hours of operation, and activities. Consider browsing their websites before calling. Also keep in mind that the staff members can handle detailed queries more effectively when they are in written form.

Books on U.S. History

The following books offer a starting point for learning more about American history and your family's place in it. Most of the books should be readily available at your local public library and your school's library. If you want to know more about a particular topic, be sure to consult the "suggestions for further reading" section found in many of the books. The reference librarian at your local library will also be able to make recommendations.

America: A Narrative History by David Emory Shi and George B. Tindall. 5th ed. (W.W. Norton and Co., 1999). This textbook weaves together political, social, cultural, and economic history to explore themes that are central to the story of the United States.

American History: A Survey by Alan Brinkley, Robert Brinkley, Frank Freidel, and T. Harry Williams. 9th ed. (McGraw-Hill, 1997). This textbook provides a thorough discussion of major events, politics, government, and diplomacy, while giving equal attention to social and cultural developments.

A Concise History of the American Republic by Samuel Eliot Morison, William Leuchtenburg, Henry Steele Commager. 2nd ed. (Oxford University Press, 1983). This compact account of U.S. history charts the course of the nation from the arrival of the Native Americans' Siberian forebears to the Carter and Reagan administrations.

Encyclopedia of American Facts and Dates by Gorton Carruth. 10th ed. (Harper and Row, 1997). This volume offers more than 15,000 entries indexed by date and subject spanning 1,000 years of U.S. history. Included are entries on exploration and settlement, wars, government, civil rights, arts, culture, business and industry, science, education, religion, fashion, and sports.

Encyclopedia of American History by Richard B. Morris and Jeffrey B. Morris, eds. 7th ed. (Harper Collins, 1996). This updated edition of a classic reference work covers the history of the United States from pre-Columbian times through the first year of the Clinton administration. It includes a basic chronology, a topical chronology, and biographies of 450 notable Americans.

Eyes of the Nation: A Visual History of the United States by Vincent Virga and the Curators of the Library of Congress. Historical commentary by Alan Brinkley (Alfred A. Knopf, 1997). Images from the collections of the Library of Congress, including prints, drawings, photographs, maps, and manuscripts, are used to construct a visual history of the United States. Brinkley's commentary explores the historical themes evoked by the images.

Historical Atlas of the United States by the National Geographic Society (National Geographic Society, 1994). Illustrations, timelines, and tables accompany topical maps that tell the story of America, including a historical approach to nontraditional subjects such as meteorology and natural disasters.

A History of US by Joy Hakim. 10 vols. (Oxford University Press, 1994). Volume 1: The First Americans; Vol. 2: Making Thirteen Colonies; Vol. 3: From Colonies to Country; Vol. 4: The New Nation; Vol. 5: Liberty for All?; Vol. 6: War, Terrible War; Vol. 7: Reconstruction and Reform; Vol. 8: An Age of Extremes; Vol. 9: War, Peace, and All that Jazz; and Vol. 10: All the People. Intended for children and teenagers, the series can also be used by adults interested in a fun and thought-provoking approach to learning American history.

A People and a Nation: A History of the United States by Mary Beth Norton, David Katzman, Paul D. Escott, Howard P. Chudacoff, Thomas G. Paterson and William M. Tuttle. 5th ed. (Houghton Mifflin Company, 1987-8). This textbook offers a compelling survey of American history that emphasizes not only political history, but also social and cultural history.

The Reader's Companion to American History by Eric Foner and John A. Garraty, eds. (Boston: Houghton Mifflin Company, 1991). This encyclopedia offers up-to-date articles on major themes, important historical events, and notable people in American history.

The Timetables of American History by Laurence Urdang, Arthur Meier Schlesinger, Jr., and Henry Steele Commager (Touchstone Books, 1996). Encompassing events from the landing of the Norsemen in 1000 A.D. through 1994, this book provides a chronology of events in American history and relates them to simultaneous developments throughout the world.

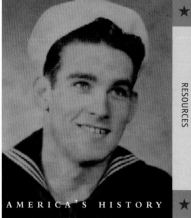

The sampling of books below encompass stories about the experiences of individuals and rich portraits of American families. Some are narratives, while others are collections of oral histories, letters, and documents. The books offer an opportunity to see how some Americans were influenced by and responded to social, cultural, and economic circumstances throughout our country's history. They also offer a starting point for you to think about how your family story may fit the larger panorama of American history.

America's Adopted Son: The Remarkable Story of an Orphaned Immigrant Boy *by Samuel Nakasian (Bookwrights Press, 1997).*

Following the massacre of his Armenian village and death of his father, Samuel Nakasian and his family emigrated to the U.S. in 1915. After the death of his mother, he became a ward of the Children's Aid Society and was placed at the Brace Farm School. Nakasian relates how he transcended overwhelming circumstances to become one of America's "adopted sons."

Ancestors: A Family History *by William Maxwell (Vintage Books, 1995).* For

years, William Maxwell's family took sepia-toned photographs as evidence of aristocratic origins, until he began to ask questions about his bloodlines. Instead, Maxwell discovered that he came from a long line of ordinary folks—itinerant preachers, farmers, small businessmen, and trailblazers.

The Color of Water: A Black Man's Tribute to His White Mother *by James McBride (Riverhead Books, 1996).*

James McBride recounts his lifelong quest to understand his mother. A Polish immigrant and the daughter of an orthodox Jewish rabbi, Rachel McBride married a black man in 1942, became the only white resident of Harlem's Red Hook Projects, founded a church, and put twelve children through college.

Coming of Age in Mississippi *by Anne Moody (1968; rev. ed. Laureleaf, 1997).*

In this classic memoir of the Civil Rights Movement, Anne Moody chronicles her childhood in Mississippi and the powerful impact the lynching of fourteen-year-old Emmett Till had on her life. She also describes her subsequent involvement in sit-ins and voter registration drives, and the worry her activism caused her family.

Ellis Island Interviews: In Their Own Words *by Peter Morton Coan (Facts on File, 1997).* This book represents a thirty-year effort by Ellis Island employees to collect the oral testimony of men and women who passed through the immigration station on their way to a new life in America. It features stories from more than 130 immigrants from Europe and the Middle East.

Families and Freedom: A Documentary History of African-American Kinship in the Civil War Era *by Ira Berlin and Leslie Rowland (Free Press, 1997).* Personal testimony and other documents were culled from Army and Freedmen's Bureau records at the National Archives to illuminate the meaning of freedom for African American families during the Civil War era.

Family *by Ian Frazier (Farrar, Straus, and Giroux, 1994).* Ian Frazier combines history, genealogy, and autobiography to tell the story of his ancestors from the Puritan settlement of the 1630s to the present. Extensive research allows him to unravel family myths and tie his family history to the ups and downs of a developing nation.

The Good War: An Oral History of World War Two *by Studs Terkel, Andre Schiffrin, ed. (rev. ed. New Press, 1997).* Journalist Studs Terkel gathers the reminiscences of 121 participants of World War II. Told by the famous and ordinary, the stories paint a vivid picture of the war and touch upon issues such as the growth of the military-industrial complex, racism, and the importance of camaraderie.

Growing Up *by Russell Baker (New American Library, 1991).* In his Pulitzer Prize-winning autobiography, Russell Baker chronicles family struggles and what it was like growing up during the 1930s and 1940s in the backwoods of Virginia, a New Jersey commuter town, and Baltimore.

Hard Times: An Oral History of the Great Depression *by Studs Terkel (1970; rev. ed. Pantheon Books, 1986).* In this book, Terkel talks to both well-known and humble Americans who lived through the Great Depression of the 1930s. The interviews capture both the somber mood and the light-hearted moments of a difficult period in American history.

Homelands and Waterways: The American Journey of the Bond Family, 1846-1926 *by Adele Logan Alexander (Pantheon Books, 1999).* As a child, Adele Logan Alexander was fascinated by stories about her great-grandfather, John Robert Bond. The son of an Irish woman and man of African ancestry, Bond immigrated to the United States during the Civil War determined to fight against slavery. Alexander traces Bond's story and those of his descendants.

RESOURCES

Homesteading: A Montana Family Album *by Percy Wollaston (Penguin, 1999).* Written for his grandchildren, Percy Wollaston's memoir portrays his parents' struggle to carve out a life on the Montana frontier at the turn-of-the century. The harsh climate, which made farming difficult, forced many settlers to abandon their dreams.

La Partera: The Story of a Midwife *by Fran Leeper Buss. (University of Michigan Press, 1980).* Fran Leeper Buss pieces together interviews to tell the story of Jesusita Aragon —a midwife who spent her life on the plains of northeastern New Mexico. Aragon's life provides a window into family and community in the American southwest.

The Last Fine Time *by Verlyn Klinkenborg (Alfred A. Knopf, 1991).* Verlyn Klinkenborg traces the Wenzek family from its emigration to turn-of-the-century New York to son Eddie's conversion of a workingman's tavern in East Buffalo into a night club serving highballs and French-fried shrimp to men and women serving in World War II.

Legacy: The Story of Talula Gilbert Bottoms and Her Quilts *by Nancilu Burdick (Rutledge Hill Press, 1988).* Talula Bottoms's quilts were family gifts—every grandchild had at least one. Inspired by her grandmother, Nancilu Burdick uses the quilts, letters, and a memoir written by Talula at the age of eighty

to write a family history that offers insights into Reconstruction Georgia, courtship and marriage, and life on an Alabama farm.

Lemon Swamp and Other Places: A Carolina Memoir *by Mamie Garvin Fields and Karen Fields. (The Free Press, 1983).* Karen Fields uses letters dating from the 1890s and interviews with her 90-year old grandmother, Mamie Garvin Fields, to reconstruct Mamie's life as an educated black woman in early 20th century Charleston, her civil rights activism, and summers on her grandfather's plantation.

Letters of a Nation: A Collection of Extraordinary American Letters *by Andrew Carroll (Broadway Books, 1997).* More than 200 letters record the history of the United States since 1630, including the first impressions of English, Irish, Chinese, and Russian immigrants on their arrival in the United States, a soldier's horror after liberating a concentration camp, and expressions of love and friendship from public figures such as Thomas Jefferson, Robert E. Lee, Ronald Reagan, and Thomas Wolfe.

Madonna Swan: A Lakota Woman's Story *by Mark St. Pierre (University of Oklahoma Press, 1991).* Over the course of six years, Madonna Swan shared the stories of three generations of Lakota women with Mark St. Pierre. Born on the Cheyenne River Reservation in 1928, Swan describes

adjustment to reservation life, a battle with tuberculosis, work as a jeweler, and ten years as a Head Start teacher.

A Midwife's Tale: The Life of Martha Ballard, Based on Her Diary, 1785-1812 *by Laurel Thatcher Ulrich (Vintage Books, 1991).* Laurel Thatcher Ulrich uses the diaries of Martha Ballard, a midwife in eighteenth-century Maine, to create an intimate history of the medical practices, family relationships, religious squabbles, and social mores of the New England frontier.

Modern American Memoirs *by Annie Dillard and Cort Conley, eds. (Harper Collins, 1995).* The book features excerpts from 35 notable memoirs, including those by Wallace Stegner, Frank Conroy, Richard Selzer, James Baldwin, Margaret Mead, and Maxine Hong Kingston. The anthology provides a glimpse at a range of American experiences and celebrates the art of autobiography.

The Names: A Memoir *by N. Scott Momaday (University of Arizona Press, 1976).* N. Scott Momaday describes his childhood and adolescence spent with his father's tribe in Oklahoma and on Navajo reservations. He weaves together tales about his mother's white and Cherokee ancestors and discusses the impact of World War II, Hollywood movies, and American education on Native American life.

On Gold Mountain: The One-Hundred Year Odyssey of My Chinese American Family *by Lisa See (Vintage Books, 1996).* Using stories from her childhood in Los Angeles' Chinatown and interviews with more than 100 family members, journalist Lisa See documents the history of her Chinese American family.

Prairie Voices: Iowa's Pioneering Women *by Glenda Riley, ed. (Iowa State University Press, 1996).* This collection brings together diaries and memoirs written by women who helped settle Iowa. The documents, which date from the 19th and 20th centuries, illustrate how these women created homes and established communities on the western frontier.

Rain of Gold *by Victor E. Villaseñor (Dell, 1992).* Novelist Victor Villaseñor tells the story of his family's immigration to, and subsequent life in, California following the Mexican revolution. Using public documents and interviews, Villaseñor follows the struggles of three generations and learns the truth behind oft-told family stories.

Remembering Ahanagran: Storytelling in a Family's Past *by Richard White (Hill and Wang, 1998).* Richard White weaves together stories told by his mother, Sara Walsh White, of her life in west Ireland, experiences as an immigrant, and the struggle to become an American. By placing his mother's stories in historical context, White shows how memory and history reinforce and challenge each other.

A Romantic Education *by Patricia Hampl (1981; 1992; W.W. Norton, 1999, with a new afterword).* Hampl's book reads as part memoir, part travelogue, and part voyage of discovery as she recounts her Midwestern childhood, coming of age during a time of protest, and her journey to communist Czechoslovakia to uncover her family's Czech-American heritage.

Roots *by Alex Haley (Doubleday, 1976).* Beginning in 1750 with Kunta Kinte's birth in an African village, the story ends seven generations later at the funeral of the author's father, a professor at the University of Arkansas. Told in vivid and engaging detail, Haley's account of his family's history has inspired millions white and black Americans to trace their roots.

A Scattered People: An American Family Moves West *by Gerald McFarland (University of Massachusetts, 1985).* Gerald McFarland's mother, Marguerite Brown, was born in 1900 in California. Using his mother's ancestors as a springboard, he traces the westward movement of several families who were eventually united in marriage.

The Schramm Letters *by Jacob Schramm, trans. and ed. by Emma S. Vonnegut (1935; 1975; Indianapolis Historical Society, 1991).* In letters to this brothers and sisters in Germany, Jacob Schramm recounts the difficulties of immigration, building a farm, and establishing community life in an English-speaking country. The letters, which read like a travelogue, were first published in German in 1837.

Skookum: An Oregon Pioneer Family's History and Love *by Shannon Applegate (William Morrow, 1988).* Shannon Applegate relates the travails of her pioneering ancestors: months on the Oregon Trail, the harsh labor of settling the frontier, encounters with prospectors, and troubled relations with Indians. Applegate celebrates the women in her family, especially as preservers of journals, diaries, and artifacts.

Slaves in the Family *by Edward Ball (Random House, 1998).* A descendant of one of the oldest slaveholding families of the South, Edward Ball began looking into his family's past after attending a reunion. To the dismay of many family members, he uncovered ties to African Americans whose ancestors were the children of liaisons between slaveowners and slaves. The book recounts the their common ancestry and Ball's encounters with all of his kin, white and black.

Somerset Homecoming: Recovering a Lost Heritage *by Dorothy Spruill Redford (Doubleday, 1988).* Dorothy Redford creates a seamless narrative of personal discovery, research, and stories of enslavement and emancipation in North Carolina that culminates in a family reunion the Somerset Plantation, where her ancestors lived as slaves.

Songs My Mother Sang to Me: An Oral History of Mexican American Women *by Patricia Preciado Martin (University of Arizona Press, 1992).* This collection captures the voices of ten Chicano women who articulate daily rhythms, expectations, and cultural practices of long-established communities in farming and mining towns of Arizona.

'Tis: A Memoir *by Frank McCourt (Scribners, 1999).* McCourt tells the classic immigrant success story: when he returned to New York in 1949 after a childhood spent in Ireland, the 19-year-old McCourt had no high school education. Within ten years, he was teaching high school in New York City. McCourt tempers the make-good tale with a harrowing account of overcoming economic obstacles and sharp observations about American society.

Wait Till Next Year: A Memoir *by Doris Kearns Goodwin (Touchstone Books, 1998).* At the center of this story about her childhood and her parents' struggles is Doris Kearns Goodwin's love of the Brooklyn Dodgers. Against the backdrop of New York baseball's glory days in the 1950s, she touches on more solemn events of the era including McCarthyism, the polio scare, and the Little Rock Nine.

The World Rushed In: The California Gold Rush Experience *by J.S. Holliday, ed. (Touchstone Books, 1981).* Editor J. S. Holliday interweaves the letters and diary of William Swain with first-hand accounts of other gold seekers in the early days of the Gold Rush. The result is a daily record of Swain's trek to California in search of gold and a glimpse into the lives of the wife, brother, and children he left behind.

The following NEH-supported documentary films explore pivotal eras in American history, as well as tell the stories of ordinary people caught up in the events of their time. The films vividly recapture the past by using a rich array of audio and visual materials, and in some cases, dramatic reenactments. On-screen interviews with historians are also a common feature. Most of the films should be available at your local library. Companion websites providing more information about the film, background history, and classroom resources have been noted where available.

Africans in America (1998) *Directed by Orlando Bagwell. Distributed by WGBH Boston Video.* This four-part series explores the economic and intellectual foundations of slavery in America and the global economy that prospered from it. The story extends from the arrival of slavery in America in the 1600s through the onset of Civil War. www.pbs.org/wgbh/aia/home.html

The Civil War (1990) *Directed by Ken Burns. Distributed by PBS Video, Time-Life Video.* This nine-part series examines the history and meaning of the Civil War, from its complex causes and the daily life of soldiers to its impact on the nation's political and social life.

Goin' to Chicago (1994) *Directed by George King. Distributed by California Newsreel.* This film chronicles the migration—in two great waves between 1917 and 1990—of more than six million African Americans from the rural South to cities in the North and West, the urban culture that resulted, and the personal toll of such a move.

The Great Depression (1993) *Executive Producer Henry Hampton. Distributed by PBS Video.* Emphasizing the stories of ordinary people, this seven-part series examines the effects of the economic depression that followed the stock market crash of 1929 and dominated the period between the two world wars.

The Great War and the Shaping of the 20th Century (1997) *Directed by Carl Byker and Mitch Wilson. Distributed by PBS Video.* This eight-part series examines the impact and importance of the First World War by exploring the military and political aspects of the conflict and its ongoing social, cultural, and personal impact. www.pbs.org/greatwar/

Indian America: A Gift From the Past (1994) *Directed by Karen Thomas. Distributed by Media Resource Assoc., Inc.* This film portrays the cultural revival experienced by the Makah community of Washington state following the discovery and excavation of a 15th-century village found on their land.

Liberty! An American Revolution (1997) *Directed by Ellen Hovde and Muffie Meyer. Distributed by PBS Video.* This six-hour series tells America's greatest political story—the history of how we became a nation. Spanning from 1763 to 1789, the series traces the transformation of Americans from loyal subjects of the British king to revolutionaries, and finally, to citizens of an entirely new kind of country. www.pbs.org/ktca/liberty/

A Life Apart: Hasidism In America (1997) *Directed by Menachem Daum and Oren Rudavsky. Distributed by First Run Features.* Many Hasidim have rejected things that most Americans take for granted: public schooling, sports, and popular music. But despite their best efforts to maintain a separate culture, they have become American Hasidim.

The Life and Times of Rosie the Riveter (1980) *Directed by Connie Field. Distributed by Direct Cinema Limited, Clarity Educational Productions.* Through newsreel footage and the testimonies of five women, this film examines the experiences of the 18 million women who went to work in factories and plants during World War II.

Mary Silliman's War (1994) *Directed by Stephen Surjick. Distributed by Heritage Films.* The experience of the Silliman family during the Revolutionary War is told from Mary Silliman's point of view and based on her family's letters and the scholarship of Richard and Joy Buel.

A Midwife's Tale (1997) *Directed by Richard P. Rogers. Distributed by PBS Video.* Martha Ballard, a midwife in Maine after the American Revolution, delivered more than 800 babies while struggling against poverty, disease, domestic abuse, and social turmoil on the northern frontier of a young nation. The film weaves Ballard's story with a historian's quest to uncover her world. www.pbs.org/wgbh/amex/midwife/

One Woman, One Vote (1995) *Produced by Ruth Pollak. Distributed by PBS Video.* The film tells the story of the seventy-year struggle to win the right to vote for women in America. Culminating in the 1920 passage of the Nineteenth Amendment to the Constitution, it examines the suffrage movement's leaders, triumphs, defeats, and internal divisions.

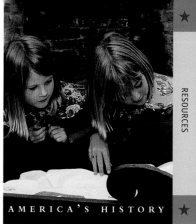

Out of Ireland (1994) *Directed by Paul Wagner. Distributed by PBS Video, Shanachie Entertainment.* Focusing on the stories of eight people, the film traces Irish immigration to America, from the famine-swept villages of nineteenth-century Ireland to the industrialized cities of twentieth-century America.

A Paralyzing Fear: The Story of Polio in America (1997*) Directed by Nina Gilden Seavey. Distributed by George Washington University.* First-person narratives from polio survivors, their families, nurses, and doctors are coupled with archival footage to create a portrait of America struggling to combat annual polio epidemics and the fear they generated.
www.pbs.org/storyofpolio/

Rebuilding the Temple: Cambodians in America (1990) *Directed by Claudia Levin and Lawrence R. Hott. Distributed by Direct Cinema Limited.* This film examines the influence of traditional Khmer Buddhism and culture on the adjustment of Cambodian refugees to life in America.

Talk to Me: Americans in Conversation (1997). *Directed by Andrea Simon. Distributed by The Cinema Guild, Inc.* This film explores Americans' shared national identity by drawing upon a wide range of American icons—from Walt Whitman and Duke Ellington to the Preamble to the Constitution and Star Trek—and through profiles of four regional communities.

The U.S.–Mexican War (1998) *Produced by Sylvia Komatsu. Distributed by PBS Video.* The four-hour film tells the story of the 1846–48 conflict in which Mexico lost almost half of its national territory—including all of the states of the present American south-west—to the United States. The film also looks at how this largely forgotten war shaped the region's identity.
www.pbs.org/kera/usmexicanwar/

Vietnam: A Television History (1983) *Executive Producer Richard Ellison. Distributed by Sony Video.* With the history of French colonial Indochina as background, this thirteen-episode series chronicles three decades of conflict in Southeast Asia, America's military involvement, and the conflicts it produced on the U.S. homefront.
www.pbs.org/wgbh/amex/vietnam/index.html

The West (1996) *Directed by Stephen Ives. Distributed by PBS Video.* This eight-part series examines the people and events that shaped the American West and untangles the myths and realities of the nation's effort to settle an uncharted wilderness and the consequences for people on both sides of the struggle.
www.pbs.org/weta/thewest/

Regional and National Resources

The following national organizations and government agencies hold records that document American history. Some of these holdings may also help to document aspects of your family's history. To learn more about the history and culture of the region in which you live, consult the regional organizations and repositories listed below. Most of them publish books and host public events that explore regional and American history. Consider browsing the websites before calling.

American Antiquarian Society
185 Salisbury Street
Worcester, MA 01609
508-755-5221
www.americanantiquarian.org

American Studies
University of New England
Westbrook College Campus
716 Stevens Avenue
Portland, ME 04103
207-283-0171
www.une.edu/

The Appalachian Center at the
University of Kentucky
624 Maxwelton Court
Lexington, KY 40506-6347
606-257-4852
www.uky.edu/rgs/appalcenter/

Balch Institute for Ethnic Studies
18 South Seventh Street
Philadelphia, PA 19106
215-925-8090
www.balchinstitute.org

Center for Great Plains Studies
University of Nebraska at Lincoln
1213 Oldfather Hall
PO Box 880314
Lincoln, NE 68588-0314
402-472-3082
www.unl.edu/plains/

Center for Greater Southwestern
Studies and the History of
Cartography
Box 19497, Central Library
University of Texas at Arlington
Arlington, TX 76019
817-272-3997
www.uta.edu/history/swstudies.htm

Center for the Study
of Southern Culture
University of Mississippi
University, MS 38677
662-915-5993
www.olemiss.edu/depts/south/

Center for the Study of the
American South
Campus Box 3355
University of North Carolina at
Chapel Hill
Chapel Hill, NC 27599-3355
919-962-5665
www.unc.edu/depts/csas/

Center for the Study of the
Southwest
Southwest Texas State University
601 University Drive
San Marcus, TX 78666
512-245-2232
www.english.swt.edu/css/
cssindex.htm

Center of the American West
University of Colorado at Boulder
Hellems 373
Campus Box 234
Boulder, CO 80309-0234
303-492-4879
www.centerwest.org/

William P. Clements Center for
Southwestern Studies
Southern Methodist University
PO Box 750176
Dallas, TX 75275-0176
www.smu.edu/~swcenter/

The David Library of the
American Revolution
1201 River Road
Route 32
PO Box 748
Washington Crossing, PA 18977
215-493-6776
www.libertynet.org/dlar/dlar.html

The Family History Library of The
Church of Jesus Christ of the
Latter-Day Saints
35 North West Temple Street
Salt Lake City, UT 84150
801-240-2331
www.familysearch.org

Immigration History
Research Center
University of Minnesota
826 Berry Street
Saint Paul, MN 55114
612-627-4208
www.umn.edu/ihrc/

Jewish Historical Society of the
Upper Midwest
Hamline University
1536 Hewitt Avenue
St Paul, MN 55104
651-523-2407
www.hamline.edu/~jhsuml

Kansas City Public Library
311 East 12th Street
Kansas City, MO 64106
816-701-3400 Ext. 2115
www.kcpl.lib.mo.us/sc/default.htm

Library of Congress
Local History and Genealogy
Reading Room
Jefferson Building
10 Independence Ave., SE
Washington, DC 20540-4660
202-707-5537
http://lcweb.loc.gov/rr/genealogy

Micronesian Area Research Center
University of Guam, UOG Station
Mangilao, GU 96923
671-7344473
http://guahan.uog.edu/marc/

Mountain West Center for
Regional Studies
0735 Old Main Hill
Utah State University
Logan UT 84322-0735
435-797-3630
www.usu.edu/~pioneers/mwc.html

National Archives and Records
Administration (NARA)
700 Pennsylvania Avenue, NW
Washington, DC 20408
202-501-5400
202-501-5404 (TTD/TTY)
www.nara.gov

National Archives at College Park
8601 Adelphi Road
College Park, MD 20740-6001
301-713-6800
www.nara.gov

NARA—Central Plains Region
2312 East Bannister Road
Kansas City, MO 64131
816-926-6272
www.nara.gov/regional/kansas.html

NARA—Central Plains Region
200 Space Center Drive
Lee's Summit, MO 64064-1182
816-478-7089
www.nara.gov/regional/
leesumit.html

NARA—Great Lakes Region
7358 South Pulaski Road
Chicago, IL 60629
773-581-7816
www.nara.gov/regional/
chicago.html

NARA—Great Lakes Region
3150 Springboro Road
Dayton, Ohio 45439-1883
937-225-2852
www.nara.gov/regional/dayton.html

NARA—Mid-Atlantic Region
900 Market Street
Philadelphia, PA 19107-4292
215-597-3000
www.nara.gov/regional/
philacc.html

NARA—New England Region
380 Trapelo Road
Waltham, MA 02452-9534
781-647-8100
www.nara.gov/regional/boston.html

NARA—New York Office
201 Varick Street
New York, NY 10014
212-337-1300
www.nara.gov/regional/
newyork.html

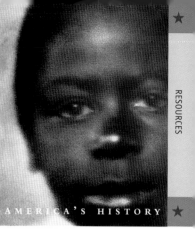

RESOURCES

NARA—Northeast Region,
Pittsfield
10 Conte Drive
Pittsfield, MA 01201-8230
413-445-6885
www.nara.gov/regional/pittsfie.html

NARA—Pacific Alaska Region
654 West Third Avenue
Anchorage, AK 99501-2145
907-271-2441
www.nara.gov/regional/
anchorag.html

NARA—Pacific Northwest
Region
6125 Sand Point Way NE
Seattle, WA 98115
206-526-6507
www.nara.gov/regional/seattle.html

NARA—Pacific Region, Laguna
Niguel
24000 Avila Road
First Floor East
Laguna Niguel, CA 92677-3497
949-360-2641
www.nara.gov/regional/laguna.html

NARA—Pacific Region, San
Francisco
1000 Commodore Drive
San Bruno, CA 94066
650-876-9009
www.nara.gov/regional/sanfranc.
html

NARA—Rocky Mountain
Region
Building 48
Denver Federal Center
PO Box 25307
Denver, CO 80225-0307
303-236-0817
www.nara.gov/regional/denver.html

NARA—Southeast Region
1557 St. Joseph Avenue
East Point, GA 30344
404-763-7477
www.nara.gov/regional/atlanta.html

NARA—Southwest Region
501 West Felix Street
Building 1
PO Box 6216
Fort Worth, TX 76115
817-334-5525
www.nara.gov/regional/ftworth.
html

National Genealogical Society
4527 17th Street North
Arlington, VA 22207-2399
703-525-0050
www.ngsgenealogy.org/

National Society of the Daughters
of the American Revolution
Library
Memorial Constitution Hall
1776 D Street, NW
Washington, DC 20006-5392
202-879-3229
www.dar.org

Naval Historical Center
Washington Navy Yard
805 Kidder Breese SE
Washington, D.C. 20374-5060
202-433-4882
www.history.navy.mil/

New England Historic
Genealogical Society
101 Newbury Street
Boston, MA 02116-3007
617-536-5740
www.nehgs.org

The New York Genealogical and
Biographical Society
122 East 58th Street
New York, NY 10022-1939
212-755-8532
www.nygbs.org

The New York Public Library
Irma and Paul Milstein Division
of U.S. History
Local History and Genealogy
Division
Room 315S
Fifth Avenue & 42nd Street
New York, NY 10018-2788
212-930-0828
www.nypl.org/research/chss/lhg/
genea.html

The Newberry Library
60 West Walton Street
Chicago, IL 60610
312-943-9090
www.newberry.org

Northwest Territory Genealogical
Society
Lewis Historical Collection Library
LRC 22
Vincennes University
Vincennes, IN 47591
812-888-4330
www.vinu.edu/lewis.htm

Rocky Mountain Jewish Historical
Society
Beck Archives/Special Collections
Penrose Library
University of Denver
2199 South University Boulevard
Denver, CO 80208
303-871-3016
www.penlib.du.edu/specoll/beck/

Smithsonian Institution
National Museum of American
History
14th Street and Constitution
Avenue, NW
Washington, DC 20506
202-357-2700
202-357-1729 (TTY)
www.si.edu/nmah/

Statue of Liberty and Ellis Island
Foundation, Inc.
Department W
52 Vanderbilt Avenue
New York, NY 10017-3898
212-833-1986
www.ellisisland.org

United States Holocaust Memorial
Museum
100 Raoul Wallenberg Place, SW
Washington, DC 20024-2126
202-488-0400
www.ushmm.org

U.S. Air Force Museum
1100 Spaatz Street
Wright-Patterson AFB, OH 45433-
7102
937-255-3284
www.wpafb.af.mil/museum/

U.S. Army Military History Institute
22 Ashburn Drive
Carlisle, PA 17013-5008
717-245-3971
http://carlisle-
www.army.mil/usamhi/

U.S. Department of the
Interior Library
1849 C Street, NW
Washington, DC 20240
202-208-5815
http://library.doi.gov

Resources in Your State

Every state and many territories have at least one of the organizations described below. These organizations can be a valuable resource for learning more about your family history and American history. Remember to use the websites to find out about collections and upcoming programs in your area.

STATE ARCHIVES
Examine official records of state governments or search for historical evidence in the documents, manuscripts, newspapers, and other materials relating to the state's history.

STATE GENEALOGICAL SOCIETIES
Connect with other genealogists. Depending on the state, you might also find research facilities, individual assistance, and workshops on conducting genealogical research.

STATE LIBRARIES
Visit the state's largest public library or research the state's archives—depending on the state. State libraries vary greatly; a few are administrative agencies that oversee public libraries in the state.

STATE HISTORICAL SOCIETIES
Take in an exhibition or attend a program or workshop on family or state history. You might also be able to research collections of manuscripts, photographs, audiovisual materials, and archaeological and historical objects relating to the state's history.

STATE HUMANITIES COUNCILS
Check to see what public education programs on family, community or state and national history are being offered.

STATE MUSEUMS
Explore your state's history. The museums are responsible for collecting, maintaining, and exhibiting archaeological and historical objects pertaining to the state's history. The state museum is often part of the state historical society.

ALABAMA
Alabama Department of Archives and History
624 Washington Avenue
PO Box 300100
Montgomery, AL 36130-0100
334-242-4435
www.archives.state.al.us

Alabama Genealogical Society
AGS Depository and Headquarters
Samford University Library
Box 2296
800 Lakeshore Drive
Birmingham, AL 35229-0001
205-726-2749
http://davisweb.samford.edu/about/special.shtml

Alabama Humanities Foundation
2217 10th Court South
Birmingham, AL 35205
205-930-0540
www.bham.net/ahf/

Alabama Public Library Service
6030 Monticello Drive
Montgomery, AL 36130
334-213-3900
334-213-3905 (TTD/TTY)
www.apls.state.al.us

Birmingham Public Library
2100 Park Place
Birmingham, AL 35203-2794
205-226-3600
205-226-3732 (TTD/TTY)
www.bham.lib.al.us

ALASKA
Alaska Historical Society
PO Box 100299
Anchorage, AK 99510-0299
907-276-1596
www.alaska.net/~ahs/

Alaska Humanities Forum
421 West First Avenue, Suite 210
Anchorage, AK 99501
907-272-5341
www.akhf.org/

Alaska State Library
Historical Collections
State Office Building
Eighth Floor
333 Willowby Avenue

Juneau, AK 99811-0571
907-465-2925
www.educ.state.ak.us/lam/Library.html

Alaska State Museum
395 Whinier Street
Juneau, AK 99801-1718
907-465-2901
907-465-3074 (TTD/TTY)
www.educ.state.ak.us/lam/museum/asmhome.html

Consortium Library
University of Alaska, Anchorage
3211 Providence Drive
Anchorage, AK 99508-8176
907-786-1874
www.uaa.alaska.edu/ed/virtualtour/library.html

Fairbanks Genealogical Society
PO Box 60534
Fairbanks, AK 99706-0534
www.ptialaska.net/~fgs/

Sheldon Jackson Museum
104 College Drive
Sitka, AK 99835-7657
907-747-8981
907-747-7834 (TTD/TTY)
www.educ.state.ak.us/lam/museum/sjhome.html

University of Alaska, Fairbanks
Alaska & Polar Regions Department
Rasmuson Library
PO Box 756808
Fairbanks, AK 99775-6808
907-474-7261
www.uaf.edu/library/collections/apr/index.html

Z. J. Loussac Library
Municipality of Anchorage
3600 Denali Street
Anchorage, AK 99503
907-562-7323

AMERICAN SAMOA
Amerika Samoa Humanities Council
PO Box 5800
Pago Pago, American Samoa
96799
011-684-633-4870/71

Office of Archives and Records
American Samoa Government
Pago Pago, AS 96799
011-684-633-1290

ARIZONA
Arizona Department of Library Archives and Public Records
History and Archives Division
1700 West Washington
Phoenix, AZ 85007
602-542-4159
www.dlapr.lib.az.us/

Arizona Historical Society
949 East Second Street
Tucson, AZ 85719
520-628-5774
http://w3.arizona.edu/~azhist/

Arizona Humanities Council
The Ellis-Shackelford House
1242 North Central Avenue
Phoenix, AZ 85004
602-257-0335
www.azhumanities.org

Arizona State Genealogical Society
PO Box 42075
Tucson, AZ 85733-2075
www.rootsweb.com/~asgs

Arizona State Museum
Documentary Relations of the Southwest
University of Arizona
Building 26
Tucson, AZ 85721
520-621-6278
www.arizona.edu/shared/libraries.shtml#museums

Arizona State University
Department of Archives and Manuscripts
Tempe, AZ 85287-1006
480-965-4932
www.asu.edu/lib/archives/

University of Arizona Library
Special Collections
PO Box 210055
Tucson, AZ 85721-0055
520-621-6423
http://dizzy.library.arizona.edu/branches/spc/homepage/index.html

ARKANSAS

Arkansas Historic Preservation
Program
1500 Tower Building
323 Center Street
Little Rock, AR 72201
501-324-9150
www.heritage.state.ar.us/ahpp/
home.html

Arkansas Humanities Council
10816 Executive Drive
Suite 310
Little Rock, AR 72211-4383
501-221-0091
www.arkhums.org

Arkansas State Genealogical
Society
PO Box 908
Hot Springs, AR 71902-0908
501-262-4513 (after 5 pm)
www.rootsweb.com/~args

Arkansas History Commission
and State Archives
One Capital Mall
Little Rock, AR 72201
501-682-6900
www.state.ar.us/ahc/

Arkansas State Library
One Capital Mall
Fifth Floor
Little Rock, AR 72201
501-682-2550
www.asl.lib.ar.us/

Butler Center for Arkansas Studies
Central Arkansas Library System
100 Rock Street
Little Rock, AR 72201
501-918-3000
www.cals.lib.ar.us/arkansas/
about.html

Grace Keith Genealogical
Collection
Fayetteville Public Library
217 East Dickson
Fayetteville, AR 72701
501-442-2242
www.fpl-ar.org/genealogy.html

CALIFORNIA

California Association of Museums
c/o Bowers Museum of
Cultural Art
2002 North Main Street
Santa Ana, CA 92706
714-567-3645

California Council
for the Humanities
312 Sutter Street
Suite 601
San Francisco, CA 94108
415-391-1474
www.calhum.org

California Genealogical
Society, Inc.
1611 Telegraph Avenue
Suite 200
Oakland, CA 94612-2152
510-663-1358
www.calgensoc.com

California Historical Society
678 Mission Street
San Francisco, CA 94105
415-357-1848
www.calhist.org

California State Archives
Division of the Secretary of
State's Office
1020 O Street
Sacramento, CA 95814
916-653-7715
www.ss.ca.gov/archives/
archives.htm

California State Library
California History Room
Room 200
900 N Street
Sacramento, CA 94237-0001
916-654-0176
www.library.ca.gov

Los Angeles Public Library
History and Genealogy
Department
630 West Fifth Street
Los Angeles, CA 90071
213-228-7000
www.lapl.org/central/history.html

COLORADO

Colorado Endowment
for the Humanities
Suite 101
1490 Lafayette Street
Denver, CO 80218
www.ceh.org

Colorado Genealogical Society
PO Box 9218
Denver, CO 80209-0218
303-571-1535
www.cogensoc.org/cgs/
cgs-home.htm

Colorado State Archives
Room 1B
1313 Sherman Street
Denver, CO 80203
303-866-2358
www.archives.state.co.us/
index.html

Colorado State Publications
Library
201 East Colfax Avenue
Denver, CO 80203
303-866-6725
www.cde.state.co.us/cdelib/
slstpubs.htm

Denver Public Library
Western History/Genealogy
Department
10 West 14th Avenue Parkway
Denver, CO 80204-2731
303-640-6291
www.denver.lib.co.us/

Stephen H. Hart Library
Colorado Historical Society
1300 Broadway
Denver, CO 80203
303-866-2305
www.gtownloop.com/chs.html

CONNECTICUT

Center for Oral History
Thomas J. Dodd Research Center
University of Connecticut
405 Babbidge Road, U-205
Storrs, CT 06269-1205
860-486-4578
www.oralhistory.uconn.edu

Connecticut Historical Society
One Elizabeth Street
Hartford, CT 06105
860-236-5621
www.chs.org

Connecticut Humanities Council
955 South Main Street
Suite E
Middletown, CT 06457
860-685-2260
www.cthum.org

Connecticut State Library
History and Genealogy Unit
231 Capital Avenue
Hartford, CT 06106
860-566-3690
www.cslib.org

Connecticut Society of
Genealogists Incorporated
PO Box 435
Glastonbury, CT 06033-0435
860-569-0002
www.csginc.org

Godfrey Memorial Library
134 Newfield Street
Middletown, CT 06457
860-346-4375
www.godfrey.org

New Haven Colony Historical
Society
114 Whitney Avenue
New Haven, CT 06510
203-562-4183

DELAWARE

Delaware Public Archives
Hall of Records
121 Duke of York Street
Dover, DE 19901
302-739-5318
www.archives.lib.de.us/index.htm

Delaware Genealogical Society
505 Market Street Mall
Wilmington, DE 19801-3091
http://delgensoc.org

Delaware State Museums
102 South State Street
PO Box 1401
Dover, DE 19901
302-739-5316
www.destatemuseums.org/

Historical Society of Delaware
505 Market Street
Wilmington, DE 19801
302-655-7161
www.hsd.org/

DISTRICT OF COLUMBIA
District of Columbia
Public Library
901 G Street, NW
Room 307
Washington, DC 20001
202-727-1213
www.dclibrary.org/washingtoniana

Historical Society of
Washington, DC
1307 New Hampshire Ave., NW
Washington, DC 20036
202-785-2058
www.hswdc.org

Howard University
Moorland-Spingarn
Research Center
500 Howard Place, NW
Washington, DC 20059
202-806-7239
www.founders.howard.edu/
moorland-spingarn/

Humanities Council of
Washington, DC
Suite 902
1331 H Street, NW
Washington, DC 20005
202-347-1732
www.humanities-wdc.org

FLORIDA
Florida Division of Historical
Resources
R.A. Gray Building
500 South Bronough Street
Tallahassee, FL 32399-0250
850-488-1480
www.flheritage.com

Florida Historical Society
1320 Highland Avenue
Melbourne, FL 32935
407-690-1971
www.florida-historical-soc.org/

Florida Humanities Council
1725-1/2 East Seventh Avenue
Tampa, FL 33605
813-272-3473
www.flahum.org

Florida State Archives
R.A. Gray Building
500 South Bronough Street
Tallahassee, FL 32399-0250
850-487-2073
http://dlis.dos.state.fl.us/barm/
fsa.html

Florida State Genealogical Society
PO Box 10249
Tallahassee, FL 32302-2249
www.rootsweb.com/~flsgs/

Museum of Florida History
500 South Bronough Street
Tallahassee, FL 32399-0250
850-488-1484
http://dhr.dos.state.fl.us/museum

GEORGIA
Atlanta History Center
130 West Paces Ferry Road, NW
Atlanta, GA 30305-1366
404-814-4000
www.atlhist.org/

Georgia Department of History
and Archives
330 Capital Avenue, SE
Atlanta, GA 30334
404-656-2393
www.sos.state.ga.us/archives/

Georgia Genealogical Society
PO Box 54575
Atlanta, GA 30308-0575
770-475-4404
www.america.net/~ggs/index.htm

Georgia Historical Society
501 Whitaker Street
Savannah, GA 31499-2001
912-651-2128
www.georgiahistory.com

Georgia Humanities Council
50 Hurt Plaza, SE
Suite 1565
Atlanta, GA 30303-2915
404-523-6220
www.emory.edu/GHC

Office of Public Library Services
Georgia Collection
156 Trinity Ave., S.W., Room 106
Atlanta, GA 30303
404-657-6229
www.public.lib.ga.us/

GUAM
Department of Parks and
Recreation
Historic Resources Division
Building 13-8 Tiyan
PO Box 2950
Agana, GU 96932
671-475-6290
www.gov.gu/dpr/hrdhome.html

Guam Humanities Council
PO Box 24854
GMF, GU 96921
671-477-4461

Guam Museum
PO Box 2950
Agana, GU 96932
671-475-4228

Nieves M. Flores Memorial
Library
254 Martyr Street
Hagatna, GU 96910-0254
671-475-4753

HAWAI`I
ALU LIKE
Native Hawai`ian Library
567 South King Street
Suite 400
Honolulu, HI 96813-3036
808-535-6750
www.alulike.org

Bernice Pauahi Bishop Museum
1525 Bernice Street
Honolulu, HI 96817
808-848-4148
www.bishopmuseum.org

Hawai`i Committee for the
Humanities
First Hawaiian Bank Building
Room 23
3599 Waialae Avenue
Honolulu, HI 96816
808-732-5402
www.planet-hawaii.com/hch

Hawai`ian Historical Society
560 Kawaiahao Street
Honolulu, HI 96813
808-537-6271
www.hawaiianhistory.org

Hawai`i State Archives
Department of Accounting and
General Services
Iolani Palace Grounds
Honolulu, HI 96813
808-586-0329
http://kumu.icsd.hawaii.gov/dags/
archives/welcome.html

IDAHO
Idaho Genealogical Society
4620 Overland Road, #204
Boise, ID 83705-2867
208-384-0542

Idaho Humanities Council
217 West State Street
Boise, ID 83702
208-345-5346
www.state.id.us/ihc/ihc.htm

The Idaho State Historical Society
Library and Archives
450 North Fourth Street
Boise, ID 83702
208-334-3356
www2.state.id.us/ishs/index.html

ILLINOIS
Chicago Historical Society
Clark Street at North Avenue
Chicago, IL 60614
Voice: 312-642-4600
Fax: 312-266-2077
www.chicagohs.org/

Illinois Humanities Council
203 North Wabash Avenue
Suite 2020
Chicago, IL 60601-2417
312-422-5580
www.PRAIRIE.org

Illinois State Archives
M.C. Norton Building
Springfield, IL 62756
217-782-4682
www.sos.state.il.us/

Illinois State Genealogical Society
P.O. Box 10195
Springfield, IL 62791-0195
217-789-1968
www.tbox.com/isgs/

Illinois State Historical Society
One Old State Capital Plaza
Springfield, IL 62701-1503
217-525-2781
www.prairienet.org/ishs/

Illinois State Library
300 South Second Street
Springfield, IL 62701-1796
217-785-5600
217-524-1137 (TTD/TTY)
www.library.sos.state.il.us/

Illinois State Museum
Spring and Edwards Streets
Springfield, IL 62706
217-782-7386
www.museum.state.il.us

INDIANA
Commission on Public Records
Indiana State Archives
W472
402 West Washington Street
Indianapolis, IN 46204
317-232-3373
www.state.in.us/icpr

Historical Genealogical
Department
Allen Country Public Library
900 Webster Street
PO Box 2270
Fort Wayne, IN 46801-2270
219-421-1225
219-424-2978 (TTD/TTY)
www.acpl.lib.in.us

Indiana Genealogical Society, Inc.
PO Box 10507
Fort Wayne, IN 46852-0507
www.indgensoc.org

Indiana Historical Bureau
140 North Senate Avenue
Indianapolis, IN 46204-2296
317-232-2535
317-232-7763 (TTY/TTD)
www.statelib.lib.in.us/

Indiana Historical Society
450 West Ohio Street
Indianapolis, IN 46202-3269
317-232-1882
317-233-6615 (TTD/TTY)
www.indianahistory.org

Indiana Humanities Council
1500 North Delaware Street
Indianapolis, IN 46202-2419
317-638-1500
www.ihc4u.org

Indiana State Library
Genealogy Division
140 North Senate Avenue
Indianapolis, IN 46204
317-232-3675
317-232-7763 (TTD/TTY)
www.statelib.lib.in.us

Indiana State Museum and
Historic Sites
202 North Alabama Street
Indianapolis, IN 46204
317-232-1637
www.state.in.us/ism

Oral History Research Center
Indiana University
Ashton-Aley 264
Bloomington, IN 47405
812-855-2856
www.indiana.edu/~ohrc/

IOWA
Humanities Iowa
100 Oakdale Northlawn
Iowa City, IA 52242-5000
319-335-4153
www.uiowa.edu/~humiowa/

Iowa Genealogical Society
PO Box 7735
Des Moines, IA 50322-7735
515-276-0287
www.digiserve.com/igs/igs.htm

State Historical Society of Iowa
Library and Archives
402 Iowa Avenue
Iowa City, IA 52240-1806
319-335-3916
www.culturalaffairs.org/shsi/
library/library.htm

State Historical Society of Iowa
600 East Locust
Des Moines, IA 50319-0290
515-281-6412
www.culturalaffairs.org/shsi

KANSAS
Kansas Collection
Spencer Research Library
University of Kansas
Lawrence, KS 66045
785-864-4274
www.ukans.edu/%7Espencer/
kc-home.htm

Kansas Genealogical Society, Inc.
Village Square Mall, Lower Level
2601 Central Ave.
PO Box 103
Dodge City, KS 67801
316-225-1951
www.dodgecity.net/kgs/

Kansas History Center
Kansas State Historical Society
Archives and Museum
6425 SW Sixth Avenue
Topeka, KS 66615
785-272-8681
785-272-8683 (TTD/TTY)
www.kshs.org

Kansas Humanities Council
112 South West Sixth Avenue
Suite 210
Topeka, KS 66603-3895
785-357-0359
www.ukans.edu/kansas/khc/
mainpage.html

Kansas State Library
Third Floor Statehouse
Topeka, KS 66612
785-296-3296
http://skyways.lib.ks.us/kansas/
KSL/

KENTUCKY
The Filson Club Historical
Society
1310 South Third Street
Louisville, KY 40208
502-635-5083
www.filsonclub.org

Kentucky Genealogical Society
PO Box 153
Frankfort, KY 40602
http://members.aol.com/
bdharney2/kgs/bh3.htm

Kentucky Historical Society
100 West Broadway
Frankfort, KY 40601
502-564-1792
www.state.ky.us/agencies/khs

Kentucky Humanities Council
206 East Maxwell Street
Lexington, KY 40508
606-257-5932
www.kyhumanities.org

Kentucky State Archives
Public Records Division
Department for Libraries
and Archives
300 Coffee Tree Road
PO Box 537
Frankfort, KY 40602-0537
502-564-8300
www.kdla.net

LOUISIANA
Louisiana Endowment
for the Humanities
225 Baronne Street
Suite 1414
New Orleans, LA 70112-1709
504-523-4352
www.leh.org

Louisiana Genealogical and
Historical Society
PO Box 82060
Baton Rouge, LA 70884-2060
http://cust2.iamerica.net/mmoore
/lghs.htm

Louisiana State Archives
3851 Essen Lane
Baton Rouge, LA 70809-2137
225-922-1208
www.sec.state.la.us/arch-1.htm

Louisiana State Museum
751 Chartres Street
PO Box 2448
New Orleans, LA 70116
504-568-6968
http://lsm.crt.state.la.us/

State Library of Louisiana
701 North Fourth Street
PO Box 131
Baton Rouge, LA 70802
225-342-4914
http://smt.state.lib.la.us

MAINE
Maine Folklife Center
5773 South Stevens Hall
University of Maine
Orono, ME 04469-5773
207-581-1891
www.umaine.edu/folklife/

Maine Genealogical Society
P.O. Box 221
Farmington, ME 04938-0221
www.rootsweb.com/~megs/
MaineGS.htm

Maine Historical Society
Center for Maine History
485 Congress Street
Portland, ME 04101
207-774-1822
www.mainehistory.org

Maine Humanities Council
371 Cumberland Avenue
PO Box 7202
Portland, ME 04112
207-773-5051
www.mainehumanities.org

Maine State Archives
84 State House Station
Augusta, ME 04333-0084
207-287-5788
www.state.me.us/sos/arc/general/
admin/mawww001.htm

Maine State Library
Cultural Building
64 State House Station
Augusta, ME 04333-0064
207-287-5600
207-287-5622 (TTD/TTY)
www.state.me.us/msl

MARYLAND
Maryland Genealogical Society
201 West Monument Street
Baltimore, MD 21201-4674
410-685-3750, Ext. 360
www.rootsweb.com/~mdsgs

Maryland Historical Society
201 West Monument Street
Baltimore, MD 21201
410-685-3750
www.mdhs.org

Maryland Humanities Council
601 North Howard Street
Baltimore, MD 21201-4585
410-625-4830
www.mdhc.org

Maryland State Archives
Hall of Records
350 Rowe Boulevard
Annapolis, MD 21401
410-260-6400
www.mdarchives.state.md.us/msa/
homepage/html/visitor.html

Maryland State Library
Resource Center
Enoch Pratt Free Library
400 Cathedral Street
Baltimore, MD 21201
410-396-5358
www.pratt.lib.md.us

MASSACHUSETTS
Historical Deerfield-Pocumtuck
Valley
Memorial Association Libraries
Six Memorial Street
PO Box 53
Deerfield, MA 01342
413-774-5581
www.historic-deerfield.org/
libraries.html

Massachusetts Archives
Reference Desk
220 Morrissey Boulevard
Boston, MA 02125
617-727-2816
www.state.ma.us./sec/arc/

Massachusetts Foundation
for the Humanities
125 Walnut Street
Watertown, MA 02472
617-923-1678
www.mfh.org

Massachusetts Genealogical
Council
PO Box 5393
Cochituate, MA 01778

Massachusetts Historical Society
1154 Boylston Street
Boston, MA 02215
617-536-1608
http://masshist.org/

Springfield Library and Museums
Association
220 State Street
Springfield, MA 01103
413-263-6800
www.quadrangle.org

State Library of Massachusetts
341 State House
Boston, MA 02133
617-727-2590
617-727-0917 (TTD/TTY)
www.state.ma.us/lib

Sturgis Library
3090 Main Street
PO Box 606
Barnstable, MA 02630
508-362-6636
www.capecod.net/sturgis/

MICHIGAN
Historical Society of Michigan
2117 Washtenaw Avenue
Ann Arbor, MI 48104-4599
734-769-1828
http://atl46.atl.msu.edu/hsm.html

Library of Michigan
717 West Allegan
PO Box 30007
Lansing, MI 48909
517-373-1300
www.libofmich.lib.mi.us

Michigan Genealogical Council
PO Box 80953
Lansing, MI 48908-0953
www.geocities.com/Heartland/
Meadows/2192/

Michigan Humanities Council
119 Pere Marquette Drive
Suite 3-B
Lansing, MI 48912-1270
517-372-7770
http://mihumanities.h-net.
msu.edu/

State Archives of Michigan
717 West Allegan
Lansing, MI 48918-1837
517-373-1408
www.sos.state.mi.us/history/
archive/archive.html

MINNESOTA
Minnesota Genealogical Society
5768 Olson Memorial Highway
Golden Valley, MN 55422-5014
612-595-9347
www.mtn.org/mgs

Minnesota Historical Society
Library
345 Kellogg Boulevard, West
Saint Paul, MN 55102-1906
651-296-2143
www.mnhs.org

Minnesota Humanities
Commission
987 East Ivy Avenue
Saint Paul, MN 55106-2046
651-774-0105
www.thinkmhc.org

MISSISSIPPI
Center for Oral History and
Cultural Heritage
PO Box 5175
University of Southern Mississippi
Hattiesburg, MS 39406-5175
601-266-4574
www.dept.usm.edu/~ocach

Family Research Association
of Mississippi
PO Box 13334
Jackson, MS 39236-3334

Mississippi Department of Archives
and History
Archives and Library Division
PO Box 571
Jackson, MS 39205-0571
601-359-6850
www.mdah.state.ms.us

Mississippi Humanities Council
3825 Ridgewood Road
Room 311
Jackson, MS 39211-6463
601-982-6752
www.ihl.state.ms.us/mhc

MY HISTORY IS AMERICA'S HISTORY

Mississippi Library Commission
1221 Ellis Avenue
Jackson, MS 39289-0700
601-961-4117
601-354-7081 (TTD/TTY)
www.mlc.lib.ms.us/

MISSOURI
Missouri Historical Society
Library and Research Center
225 South Skinker Boulevard
PO Box 11940
St. Louis, MO 63112-0040
314-746-4599
www.mohistory.org

Missouri Humanities Council
911 Washington Avenue
Suite 215
St. Louis, MO 63101-1208
314-621-7705
www.umsl.edu/community/
mohuman

Missouri State Archives
Office of the Secretary of State
PO Box 778
600 West Main
Jefferson City, MO 65102
573-571-3280
http://mosl.sos.state.mo.us/
rec-man/arch.html

Missouri State Genealogical
Association
PO Box 833
Columbia, MO 65205-0833
www.umr.edu/stauter/mosga

State Historical Society of
Missouri
1020 Lowry
Columbia, MO 65201-7298
573-882-7083
www.system.missouri.edu/shs

MONTANA
Montana Committee
for the Humanities
University of Montana
311 Brandy Hall
Missoula, MT 59812-8214
406-243-6022
www.umt.edu/lastbest

Montana Historical Society
225 North Roberts Street
Harlena, MT 59620
406-444-2694
www.his.mt.gov

Missoula Public Library
301 East Main
Missoula, MT 59802-4799
406-721-2665
www.marsweb.com/~mslaplib

Montana State Genealogical
Society
PO Box 555
Chester, MT 59522
www.roosweb.com/~mtmsgs/

NEBRASKA
Library/Archives Division
Nebraska State Historical Society
PO Box 82554
1500 R Street
Lincoln, NE 68501-2554
402-471-4772
www.nebraskahistory.org

Nebraska Humanities Council
Lincoln Center Building
Suite 225
215 Centennial Mall South
Lincoln, NE 68508
402-471-2131
www.lincolnne.com/
nonprofit/nhc

Nebraska Library Commission
1200 N Street
Suite 120
Lincoln, NE 68508-2023
402- 471-2045
www.nlc.state.ne.us/

Nebraska State Genealogical
Society
PO Box 5608
Lincoln, NE 68505-0608
402-395-6586
www.rootsweb.org/~negenweb/
societies/stgnsoc.html

NEVADA
Nevada Historical Society
1650 North Virginia Street
Reno, NV 89503
775-688-1191
http://dmla.clan.lib.nv.us/

Nevada Humanities Committee
1034 North Sierra Street
PO Box 8029
Reno, NV 89507
775-784-6587
www.unr.edu/nhc

Nevada State Library and Archives
Archives and Records
100 North Stewart Street
Carson City, NV 89701-4285
775-687-5210
775-687-8338 (TTD/TTY)
www.clan.lib.nv.us

NEW HAMPSHIRE
New Hampshire Division of
Historical Resources
19 Pillsbury Street
Concord, NH 03301-2043
603-271-3483
1-800-735-2964 (TTD/TTY)
www.state.nh.us

New Hampshire Historical
Society
30 Park Street
Concord, NH 03301
603-225-3381 ext. 11
www.NHhistory.org

New Hampshire Humanities
Council
PO Box 2228
Concord, NH 03302
603-224-4071
www.nhhc.org

New Hampshire Society
of Genealogists
PO Box 2316
Concord, NH 03302-2316
603-225-3381
www.tiac.net/users/nhsog/

New Hampshire State Archives
71 South Fruit Street
Concord, NH 03301-2410
603-271-2236
www.state.nh.us/state/archives.htm

New Hampshire State Library
20 Park Street
Concord, NH 03301
603-271-2144
1-800-735-2964 (TTD/TTY)
www.state.nh.us/nhsl/

NEW JERSEY
Genealogical Society
of New Jersey
PO Box 1291
New Brunswick, NJ 08903

New Jersey Council
for the Humanities
28 West State Street
Sixth Floor
Trenton, NJ 08608
609-695-4838
www.njch.org

New Jersey Historical
Commission
PO Box 305
Trenton, NJ 08625-0530
609-292-6062
www.state.nj.us/state/history/
hisidx.html

New Jersey Historical Society
Genealogy Club
52 Park Place
Newark, NJ 07102
973-596-8500

New Jersey State Archives
185 West State Street
PO Box 307
Trenton, NJ 08625-0307
609-292-6265
www.state.nj.us/state/darm/
archives.html

New Jersey State Library
185 West State Street
PO Box 520
Trenton, NJ 08625-0520
609-292-6220
www.njstatelib.org

New Jersey State Museum
PO Box 530
205 West State Street
Trenton, NJ 08625-0530
609-292-6464
www.prodworks.com/trenton/
njsmus.htm

NEW MEXICO

New Mexico Endowment
for the Humanities
209 Onate Hall
Corner of Campus and
Girard, NE
University of New Mexico
Albuquerque, NM 87131-1213
505-277-3705
www.nmeh.org

New Mexico Genealogical Society
PO Box 8283
Albuquerque, NM 87198-8283
505-828-2514
www.nmgs.org

New Mexico Records Center
and Archives
1205 Camino Carlos Rey
Santa Fe, NM 87505
505-476-7908
www.state.nm.us/cpr/

New Mexico State Library
1209 Camino Carlos Rey
Santa Fe, NM 87505
505-476-9700
www.stlib.state.nm.us

NEW YORK

New York Council
for the Humanities
150 Broadway, Suite 1700
New York, NY 10038
212-233-1131
www.culturefront.org

New York Genealogical and
Biographical Society
122-126 East 58th Street
New York, NY 10022-1939
212-755-8532
www.nygbs.org

The New York Historical Society
170 Central Park West
New York, NY 10024-5194
212-873-3400
www.nyhistory.org

New York State Archives
Cultural Education Center
Suite 11D40
Empire State Plaza
Albany, NY 12230
518-474-8955
www.sara.nysed.gov

New York State Historical
Association Library
PO Box 800
Lake Road
Cooperstown, NY 13326
607-547-1470
www.nysha.org

New York State Library
Cultural Education Center
Empire State Plaza
Albany, NY 12230
518-474-5355
518-473-7121 (TTD/TTY)
www.nysl.nysed.gov

New York State Museum
Cultural Education Center
Empire State Plaza
Albany, NY 12230
518-474-5353
www.nysm.nysed.gov/

NORTH CAROLINA

Genealogical Services
State Library of North Carolina
109 East Jones Street
Raleigh, NC 27601
919-733-7222
http://statelibrary.dcr.state.nc.us/iss
/gr/genealog.htm

North Carolina Genealogical
Society
PO Box 1492
Raleigh, NC 27602
www.ncgenealogy.org

North Carolina Humanities
Council
425 Spring Garden Street
Greensboro, NC 27401
919-334-5325
www.nchumanities.org

North Carolina Museum
of History
Five East Edenton Street
Raleigh, NC 27601-1011
919-715-0200
www.nchistory.dcr.state.nc.us/
museums

North Carolina State Archives
and Records
109 East Jones Street
Raleigh, NC 27601-2807
919-733-3952
www.ah.dcr.state.us/sections/
archives

NORTH DAKOTA

North Dakota Humanities
Council
Suite 3
2900 Broadway East
PO Box 2191
Bismarck, ND 58502-2191
701-255-3360
www.nd-humanities.org

State Historical Society of
North Dakota
North Dakota Heritage Center
612 East Boulevard Avenue
Bismarck, ND 58505-0830
701-328-2666
www.state.nd.us/hist/

NORTHERN MARIANA
ISLANDS

Commonwealth of the Northern
Mariana Islands
Council for the Humanities
AAA-3394
PO Box 10001
Salpan, MP 96950
670-235-4785
http://cnmi.humanities.org.mp

OHIO

Ohio Genealogical Society
713 South Main Street
Mansfield, OH 44907-1644
419-756-7294
www.ogs.org

Ohio Humanities Council
695 Bryden Road
PO Box 06354
Columbus, OH 43206-0354
614-461-7802
www.ohiohumanities.org

State Archives of Ohio
c/o Ohio Historical Society
1982 Velma Avenue
Columbus, OH 43211-2497
614-297-2510
www.ohiohistory.org

State Library of Ohio
65 South Front Street
Columbus, OH 43215-2789
614-644-1972
http://winslo.state.oh.us

OKLAHOMA

Oklahoma Genealogical Society
PO Box 12986
Oklahoma City, OK 73157-2986
www.rootsweb.com/~okgs/

Oklahoma Historical Society and
State Museum of History
2100 North Lincoln Boulevard
Oklahoma City, OK 73105
405-522-5206
www.ok-history.mus.ok.us/

Oklahoma Humanities Council
Suite 270
428 West California
Oklahoma City, OK 73102
405-235-0280
www.okhumanitiescouncil.org

OREGON

Genealogical Forum of
Oregon, Inc.
2130 South West Fifth Avenue
Suite 220
Portland, OR 97201-4934
503-227-2398
www.gfo.org

Oregon Council for the
Humanities
Suite 225
812 South West Washington
Portland, OR 97205
503-241-0543
www.oregonhum.org

Oregon Genealogical Society
PO Box 10306
Eugene, OR 97440-2306
501-746-7924
www.roobsweb.com/~orlncogs/og
sinfo.htm

Oregon Historical Society at the
Oregon History Center
1200 South West Park Ave
Portland, OR 97205-2483
503-222-1741
503-306-5194 (TTD/TTY)
www.ohs.org/

Oregon State Archives
800 Summer Street NE
Salem, OR 97310
503-373-0701
http://arcweb.sos.state.or.us

Oregon State Library
250 Winter Street, NE
Salem, OR 97310
503-378-4243
503-378-4276 (TTD/TTY)
www.osl.state.or.us/oslhome.html

PENNSYLVANIA
Carnegie Library of Pittsburgh
Pennsylvania Department
4400 Forbes Avenue
Pittsburgh, PA 15213
412-622-3154
www.clpgh.org/clp/Pennsylvania

Genealogical Society of
Pennsylvania
3rd Floor
1305 Locust Street
Philadelphia, PA 19107-5405
215-545-0391
www.libertynet.org/gspa/

Historical Society of Pennsylvania
1300 Locust Street
Philadelphia, PA 19107
215-732-6200
www.libertynet.org/pahist

Historical Society of
Western Pennsylvania
1212 Smallman Street
Pittsburgh, PA 15222-4200
412-454-6364
www.pghhistory.org

Pennsylvania Humanities Council
Suite 715
325 Chestnut Street
Philadelphia, PA 19106-2607
215-925-1005
www.libertynet.org/~phc

Pennsylvania State Archives
PO Box 1026
Harrisburg, PA 17108-1026
717-783-3281
800-654-5984 (TTD/TTY)
www.phmc.state.pa.us

State Library of Pennsylvania
Corner of Commonwealth
and Walnut
PO Box 1601
Harrisburg, PA 17105-1601
717-783-5950
717-772-2863 (TTD/TTY)
www.pde.psu.edu

PUERTO RICO
Fundación Puertorriqueña de las
Humanidades
109 San Jose Street, 3rd Floor
Box 9023920
San Juan, PR 00902-3920
787-721-2087
http://premium.caribe.net/~fph

RHODE ISLAND
Rhode Island Committee
for the Humanities
60 Ship Street
Providence, RI 02903
401-273-2250
www.uri.edu/rich/

Rhode Island Genealogical
Society
PO Box 433
Greenville, RI 02828

Rhode Island Historical Society
110 Benevolent Street
Providence, RI 02906
401-331-8575
www.rihs.org

Rhode Island State Archives
337 Westminster Street
Providence, RI 02903
401-222-2353
www.state.ri.us/archives

SOUTH CAROLINA
South Carolina Archives and
History Center
8301 Parklane Road
Columbia, SC 29223-4905
803-896-6104
www.state.sc.us/scdah

South Carolina Historical Society
100 Meeting Street
Charleston, SC 29401-2299
843-723-3225
www.schistory.org

South Carolina Humanities
Council
1308 Columbia College Drive
Columbia, SC 29250
803-691-4100
www.schumanities.org

South Carolina State Library
1500 Senate Street,
PO Box 11469
Columbia, SC 29211-1469
803-734-8666
803-734-7298 (TTD/TTY)
www.state.sc.us/scsl

South Carolina State Museum
301 Gervais Street
PO Box 100107
Columbia, SC 29202-3107
803-898-4921
www.museum.state.sc.us

SOUTH DAKOTA
South Dakota Genealogical
Society
PO Box 1101
Pierre, SD 57501

South Dakota Humanities Council
PO Box 7050
University Station
Brookings, SD 57007
605-688-6113
http://web.sdstate.edu/
humanities/

South Dakota State Archives
900 Governors Drive
Pierre, SD 57501-2217
605-773-3468
www.state.sd.us/deca/cultural/
archives.htm

South Dakota State Library
900 Governors Drive
Pierre, SD 57501-2294
605-773-3131
www.state.sd.us/library

TENNESSEE
Tennessee Genealogical Society
PO Box 247
Brunswick, TN 38014
901-381-1447
www.rootsweb.com/~tngs

Tennessee Humanities Council
1003 18th Avenue South
Nashville, TN 37212
615-320-7001
www.tn-humanities.org

Tennessee State Library
and Archives
403 Seventh Avenue North
Nashville, TN 37243-0312
615-741-2764
www.state.tn.us/sos/statelib/tsla-
home.htm

TEXAS
Dallas Public Library
Texas/Dallas History and
Archives Division
1515 Young Street
Dallas, TX 75201
214-670-1435
214-670-1716 (TTD/TTY)
www.lib.ci.dallas.tx.us

Institute of Texan Cultures
801 South Bowie Street
San Antonio, TX 78205
210-458-2300
www.texancultures.utsa.edu

Texas Council for the Humanities
Banister Place A
3809 South Second Street
Austin, TX 78704-7058
512-440-1991
www.public-humanities.org

Texas State Historical Association
2/306 Richardson Hall
University Station
Austin, TX 78712
512-471-1525
www.tsha.utexas.edu

Texas State Library and Archives
Commission
Archives and Information Services
Division
Genealogy Collection
1201 Brazos Street
Austin, TX 78711
512-463-5455
www.tsl.state.tx.us/lobby

UTAH

Genealogical Society of Utah
35 Northwest Temple Street
Salt Lake City, UT 84150

Oral History Institute
56 East 300 South
Salt Lake City, UT 84111
801-355-3903

Utah Historical Society
300 Rio Grande
Salt Lake City, UT 84101
801-533-3500
www.ce.ex.state.ut.us/history/

Utah Humanities Council
202 West 300 North
Salt Lake City, UT 84103
801-359-9670
www.utahhumanities.org

Utah State Archives
Archives Building
State Capitol
PO Box 141021
Salt Lake City, UT 84114-1021
801-538-3013
www.archives_state.ut.us

Utah State Library
250 North 1950 West, Suite A
Salt Lake City, UT 84116-7901
801-715-6757
www.state.lib.ut.us/

VERMONT

Genealogical Society of Vermont
PO Box 1553
St. Albans, VT 05478-1006
http://ourworld.compuserve.com/
homepages/induni_n_j/
membersh.htm

General Services Center
Public Records Division
US Route 2,
Middlesex Drawer 33
Montpelier, VT 05633-7601
802-828-3700
www.bgs.state.vt.us/GSC/pubrec/

Vermont Council
on the Humanities
200 Park Street
Morrisville, VT 05661
802-888-3183
www.vermonthumanities.org

Vermont Folklife Center
Three Court Square
Middleburg, VT 05753
802-388-4964
www.vermontfolklifecenter.org

Vermont Historical Society
Pavilion Office Building
109 State Street
Montpelier, VT 05609-0901
802-828-2291
www.state.vt.us/vhs

Vermont State Archives
Redstone
26 Terrace Street
Drawer 9
Montpelier, VT 05609
802-828-2369
www.sec.state.vt.us/

Vermont State Library
109 State Street
Montpelier, VT 05609-0601
802-828-3261
http://dol.state.vt.us

University of Vermont
Special Collections
Bailey/Howe Library
Burlington, VT 05405
802-656-2138
www.sageunix.uvm.edu/page2.html

VIRGIN ISLANDS

Virgin Islands Humanities Council
5-6 Kongens Gade
Corbiere Complex
Suites 200B & 201B
St. Thomas, USVI 00802
340-776-4044

VIRGINIA

Library of Virginia
800 East Broad Street
Richmond, VA 23219
804-692-3500
804-692-3976 (TTD/TTY)
www.lva.lib.va.us/

Virginia Department of Historic
Resources
2801 Kensington Avenue
Richmond, VA 23219
804-367-2323
http://state.vipnet.org/dhr/
dhrwebpg.htm

Virginia Foundation
for the Humanities
145 Ednam Drive
Charlottesville, VA 22903-4629
804-924-3296
www.virginia.edu/vfh

Virginia Genealogical Society
5001 West Broad Street
Suite 115
Richmond, VA 23230-3023
804-285-8954
www.vgs.org

Virginia Historical Society
The Center for Virginia History
428 North Boulevard
PO Box 7311
Richmond, VA 23221-0311
804-358-4901
www.vahistorical.org

WASHINGTON

Humanities Department
Seattle Public Library
1000 Fourth Avenue
Seattle, WA 98104
206-386-4625
www.spl.org

Washington Commission
for the Humanities
Suite 300
615 Second Avenue
Seattle, WA 98104
206-682-1770
www.humanities.org

Washington State Archives
1129 Washington Street, SE
Olympia, WA 98504-0238
360-586-1492
www.secstate.wa.gov/archives/
main.htm

Washington State Genealogical
Society
PO Box 1422
Olympia, WA 98507-1422
www.rootsweb.com/~wasgs/

Washington State Historical
Society
Research Center
315 North Stadium Way
Tacoma, WA 98402-3109
253-798-5914
www.wshs.org/index2.htm

Washington State Historical
Society
1911 Pacific Avenue
Tacoma, WA 98402-3109
253-272-3500

Washington State Library
Washington Room
PO Box 42460
415 15th Avenue, SW
Olympia, WA 98504-2460
360-704-5209
www.statelib.wa.gov

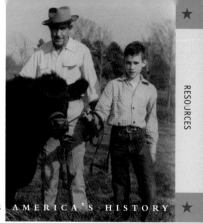

WEST VIRGINIA
West Virginia Division of Culture
and History
The Cultural Center
1900 Kanawha Boulevard East
Charleston, WV 25305-0300
304-558-0230
304-558-0220 (TTD/TTY)
www.wvlc.wvnet.edu/culture/
front.html

West Virginia Genealogical
Society, Inc.
PO Box 249
Elkview, WV 25071
304-965-1179

West Virginia Humanities Council
723 Kanahwa Boulevard, East
Suite 800
Charleston, WV 25301
304-346-8500
www.wvhc.com

WISCONSIN
Milwaukee Public Library
814 West Wisconsin Avenue
Milwaukee, WI 53233-2385
414-286-3000
414-286-3062 (TTD/TTY)
www.mpl.org

State Historical Society
of Wisconsin
816 State Street
Madison, WI 53706-1482
608-264-6535
www.shsw.wisc.edu

Wisconsin Genealogical Council,
Incorporated
1075 Kenwood Street
Green Bay, WI 54304-3804
920-494-7989

Wisconsin Humanities Council
802 Regent Street
Madison, WI 53715-2610
608-262-0706
www.danenet.wicip.org/whc/

Wisconsin State Genealogical
Society
2109 Twentieth Avenue
Monroe, WI 53566-3426
608-325-2609
www.rootsweb.com/~wsgs

WYOMING
American Heritage Center
University of Wyoming
Centennial Complex
PO Box 3924
Laramie, WY 82071-3924
307-766-4114
www.uwyo.edu/ahc

Buffalo Bill Historical Center
720 Sheridan Avenue
Cody, WY 82414
307-587-4771
www.bbhc.org

Wyoming Council
for the Humanities
PO Box 3643
University Station
Laramie, WY 82071-3643
307-766-6496
www.uwyo.edu/special/wch/

Wyoming State Historic
Preservation Office
3rd Floor
2301 Central Avenue
Cheyenne, WY 82002
307-777-7697
http://commerce.state.wy.us/CR/
SHPO

Wyoming State Library
Supreme Court and
State Library Building
2301 Capitol Avenue
Cheyenne, WY 82002-0060
307-777-6333
http://will.state.wy.us/

Places to Visit

Learn more about the history of the United States. See artifacts from the past. Walk in the steps of your ancestors. You can do all of these by visiting exhibitions funded by the National Endowment for the Humanities and by exploring historical sites operated by the National Park Service. For an updated list of exhibitions in your area funded by the NEH, visit www.neh.gov.

ALABAMA

Horseshoe Bend National Military Park
11238 Horseshoe Bend Road
Daviston, AL 36256
256-234-7111
www.nps.gov/hobe

Russell Cave National Monument
3729 County Road 98
Bridgeport, AL 35740
256-495-2672
www.nps.gov/ruca

Tuskegee Institute National Historic Site
PO Drawer 10
Tuskegee Institute, AL 36087
334-727-3200
www.nps.gov/tuin/

ALASKA

Klondike Gold Rush National Historical Park
PO Box 517
Skagway, AK 99840-0517
907-983-2921
www.nps/gov/klgo/

Northwest Alaska National Parklands
PO Box 1029
Kotzebue, AK 99752
907-442-8300
www.nps.gov/noaa/

Sitka National Historical Park: Russian Bishop's House
106 Metlakatla Street
Sitka, AK 99835-7665
907-747-6281
www.nps.gov/sitk/

ARIZONA

Bisbee Mining and Historical Museum
Exhibit: "Bisbee: Urban Outpost on the Frontier"
No. 5 Copper Queen Plaza
Bisbee, AZ 85603
520-432-7071
www.azstarnet.com/nonprofit/bisbeemuseum

Canyon de Chelly National Monument
PO Box 588
Chinle, AZ 86503
520-674-5500
www.nps.gov/cach/

Casa Grande Ruins National Monument
1100 Ruins Drive
Coolidge, AZ 85228
520-723-3172
www.nps.gov/cagr/

Coronado National Memorial
4101 East Montezuma Canyon Road
Hereford, AZ 85615
520-366-5515
www.nps.gov/coro

Heard Museum
Exhibit: "Remembering Our Indian School Days: The Boarding School Experience" (opens February 19, 2000)
22 East Monte Vista Road.
Phoenix, AZ 85004
602-252-8840
www.heard.org

Hubbell Trading Post National Historic Site
PO Box 150
Ganado, AZ 86505-0150
520-755-3475
www.nps.gov/hutr/

Montezuma Castle National Monument
PO Box 219
Camp Verde, AZ 86322
520-567-3322
www.nps.gov/moca/

Navajo National Monument
HC 71
PO Box 3
Tonalea, AZ 86044-9704
520-672-2366
www.nps.gov/nava/home.htm

Pipe Spring National Monument
HC65 PO Box 5
Fredonia, AZ 86022
520-643-7105
www.nps.gov/pisp/

Tonto National Monument
PO Box 4602
Roosevelt, AZ 85545
520-467-2241
www.nps.gov/tont/

Tumacacori National Historical Park
PO Box 67
Tumacacori, AZ 85640
520-398-2341
www.nps.gov/tuma

Tuzigoot National Monument
PO Box 219
Camp Verde, AZ 86322
520-634-5564
www.nps.gov/tuzi/

University of Arizona Museum of Art
Exhibit: "Paths of Life: American Indians of the Southwest"
Park & Speedway
Tucson, AZ 85721
520-621-7567
http://artmuseum.arizona.edu/art.html

ARKANSAS

Arkansas Museum of Discovery
Exhibit: "Arkansas Indians: Roots, Removal, Rebirth"
500 Markham
Little Rock, AR 72201
501-396-7050
www.amod.org

Arkansas Post National Monument
1741 Old Post Road
Gillett, AR 72055
870-548-2207
www.nps.gov/arpo/

Fort Smith National Historic Site
PO Box 1406
Fort Smith, AR 72902
501-783-3961
www.nps.gov/fosm/

Pea Ridge National Military Park
PO Box 700
Pea Ridge, AR 72757-0700
501-451-8122
www.nps.gov/peri

CALIFORNIA

Cabrillo National Monument
PO Box 6670
San Diego, CA 92106
619-557-5450
www.nps.gov/cabr/

Hovenweep National Monument
McElmo Route
Cortez, CA 81321
970-749-0510
www.nps.gov/hove/

Natural History Museum of Los Angeles County
Exhibit: "The Times-Mirror Hall of Native American Cultures"
900 Exposition Blvd
Los Angeles, CA 90007
213-763-3466
www.nhm.org

Port Chicago Naval Magazine National Memorial
PO Box 280
Danville, CA 94526
925-838-0249
www.nps.gov/poch/

Ventura County Museum of History and Art
Exhibit: "Ventura County in the New West"
100 East Main Street
Ventura, CA 93001
805-653-0323
www.vcmha.org

COLORADO

Bent's Old Fort National Historical Site
35110 Highway 194 East
La Junta, CO 81050
719-383-5010
www.nps.gov/beol/home.htm

Mesa Verde National Park
PO Box 8
Mesa Verde, CO 81330
970-529-4465
www.nps.gov/meve

CONNECTICUT
Institute for American
Indian Studies
Exhibits: "Interpreting the Native
American Landscape: The Long
House Room" and "As We Tell
Our Stories: Living Traditions and
the Algonkian Peoples of Southern
New England"
38 Curtis Road
Washington Green, CT 06793
860-868-0518

Weir Farm National Historic Site
735 Nod Hill Road
Wilton, CT 06897
203-834-1896
www.nps.gov/wefa/

DELAWARE
Henry Francis Dupont Winterthur
Museum
Exhibit: "Perspectives on the
Decorative Arts in Early America"
Route 52
Winterthur, DE 19735
302-888-4600
www.winterthur.org/

DISTRICT OF COLUMBIA
Frederick Douglass National
Historical Site
National Capitol Parks—East
1900 Anacostia Drive, SE
Washington, DC 20020
202-426-5961
www.nps.gov/frdo/freddoug.html

Mary McLeod Bethune Council
House
National Historical Site
1318 Vermont Ave, NW
Washington, DC 20005
202-673-2402
www.nps.gov/mamc

National Museum of American
History, Smithsonian Institution
Exhibit: "From Field to Factory:
Afro-American Migration, 1915-40"
14th St. & Constitution Ave, NW
Washington, DC 20560
202-357-2700
www.si.edu/nmah/youmus/
ex11fact.htm

Sewall–Belmont House National
Historical Site
144 Constitution Avenue, NE
Washington, DC 20002
202-546-1210
www.natwomanparty.org

FLORIDA
Castillo de San Marcos
National Monument
One South Castillo Drive
St. Augustine, FL 32084
904-829-6506
www.nps.gov/casa/

De Soto National Memorial
PO Box 15390
Bradenton, FL 34280
941-792-0458
www.nps.gov/deso/

Dry Tortugas National Park
c/o Everglades National Park
40001 State Road 9336
Homestead, FL 33034
305-242-7700
www.nps.gov/drto/

Florida Museum of
Natural History
Exhibit: "People of the Estuary:
6,000 Years in South Florida"
(opens spring 2000)
Gainesville, FL 32611
352-846-2000
www.flmnh.ufl.edu/

Fort Caroline National Memorial
12713 Fort Caroline Road
Jacksonville, FL 32225
904-641-7155
www.nps.gov/foca/

Fort Matanzas National
Monument
8635 Highway A1A South
St. Augustine, FL 32086
904-471-0116
www.nps.gov/foma/expanded/
home.htm

Mission San Luis
Exhibit: "San Luis de Apalachee:
Interpretation of a 17th-Century
Spanish Mission"
Tallahassee, FL 32399-0250
850-487-3711
www.dos.state.fl.us/dhr/bar/
san_luis/

Timucuan Ecological and Historic
Preserve
Kingsley Plantation
13165 Mount Pleasant Road
Jacksonville, FL 32225
904-641-7155
www.nps.gov/timu/

GEORGIA
Andersonville National
Historical Site
Route 1
PO Box 800
Andersonville, GA 31711
912-924-0343
www.nps.gov/ande/

Atlanta History Center
Exhibits: "Turning Point:
The American Civil War" and
"Metropolitan Frontiers: Atlanta,
1835-2000"
130 West Paces Ferry Road, NW
Atlanta, GA 30305
404-814-4000
www.atlhist.org

Chickamauga and Chattanooga
National Military Park
PO Box 2128
Fort Oglethorpe, GA 30742
706-866-9241
www.nps.gov/chch/

Fort Frederica National
Monument
Route 9, Box 286-C
St. Simons Island, GA 31522-9710
912-638-3639
www.nps.gov/fofr/vvc.htm

Jimmy Carter National
Historic Site
300 North Bond Street
Plains, GA 31780
912-824-4104
www.nps.gov/jica/

Kennesaw Mountain National
Battlefield Park
900 Kennesaw Mountain Drive
Kennesaw, GA 30152-4855
770-427-4686
www.nps.gov/kemo/

Martin Luther King, Jr. National
Historical Site
450 Auburn Avenue, NE
Atlanta, GA 30312
404-331-6922
www.nps.gov/malu/

Ocmulgee National Monument
1207 Emery Highway
Macon, GA 31217-4320
912-752-8257
www.nps.gov/ocmu/

GUAM
War in the Pacific National
Historical Park
PO Box FA
Agana, Guam 96910
671-477-9362
www.nps.gov/wapa/

HAWAI`I
Kaloko-Honokohau National
Historical Park
73-4786 Kanalani Street 14
Kailua-Kona, HI 96740-2600
808-329-6881
www.nps.gov/kaho/

Kona Historical Society
Exhibit: "Kona Coffee Farm"
PO Box 398
Captain Cook, HI 96704
808-323-3222
http://pastime2000.com/VE/
index.htm

Pu`uhonua o Honaunau National
Historical Park
PO Box 129
Honaunau, HI 96726-0129
808-328-2326
www.nps.gov/puho/

Pu`ukohola Heiau National
Historic Site
PO Box 44340
Kawaihae, HI 96743
808-882-7218
www.nps.gov/puhe/

USS Arizona Memorial
One Arizona Memorial Place
Honolulu, HI 96818-3145
808-422-2771
www.nps.gov/usar

IDAHO
Nez Perce National
Historical Park
PO Box 93
Highway 95
Spalding, ID 83540-9715
208-843-2261
www.nps.gov/nepe/

ILLINOIS
Chicago Historical Society
Exhibit: "A House Divided:
America in the Age of Lincoln"
Clark Street at North Avenue
Chicago, IL 60614-6099
312-642-4600
www.chicagohistory.org

Field Museum of Natural History
Exhibits: "Peoples of the Pacific"
and "Africa"
Roosevelt Road at Lake Shore
Drive
Chicago, IL 60605
312-922-9410
www.fmnh.org

Illinois and Michigan Canal
State Trail
402 Ottawa Street
Morris, IL 60450
815-942-9501
http://dnr.state.il.us/lands/
landmgt/parks/i&m/main.htm

Illinois State Museum
Exhibit: "At Home in the
Heartland"
Spring and Edwards Streets
Springfield, IL 62706
217-782-7387
www.museum.state.il.us/

Lincoln Home National
Historical Site
413 South Eighth Street
Springfield, IL 62701-1905
217-492-4241 x221
www.nps.gov/liho

INDIANA
George Rogers Clark National
Historical Park
401 South Second Street
Vincennes, IN 47591-1001
812-882-1776
www.nps.gov/gero/

Lincoln Boyhood National
Monument
PO Box 1816
Lincoln City, IN 47552-1816
812-937-4541
www.nps.gov/libo/

IOWA
Effigy Mounds National
Monument
151 Highway 76
Harpers Ferry, IA 52146-7519
319-873-3491
www.nps.gov/efmo/

Herbert Hoover National
Historical Site
PO Box 607
West Branch, IA 52358
319-643-2541
www.nps.gov/heho/

Mississippi River Museum
Exhibit: "Make Me a River:
Visions and Revisions of the
Upper Mississippi"
400 East 3rd Street
Dubuque, IA 52004
319-557-9545
Website debuts November 1999

KANSAS
Brown v. Board of Education
National Historic Site
424 South Kansas Avenue,
Suite 220
Topeka, KS 66603-3441
785-354-4273
www.nps.gov/brvb/

Fort Larned National Historic Site
Route 3
Larned, KS 67550-9733
316-285-6911
www.nps.gov/fols/home.html

Fort Scott National Historical Site
PO Box 918
Old Fort Boulevard
Fort Scott, KS 66701-1471
316-223-0310
www.nps.gov/fosc/home.htm

Nicodemus National Historic Site
c/o Fort Larned National
Historic Site
Route 3
Larned, KS. 67550
316-285-6911
www.nps.gov/nico/

KENTUCKY
Abraham Lincoln Birthplace
National Historical Site
2995 Lincoln Farm Road
Hodgenville, KY 42748-9707
502-358-3137
www.nps.gov/abli/linchomj.htm

Cumberland Gap National
Historical Park
PO Box 1848
Middlesboro, KY 40965-1848
606-248-2817
www.nps.gov/cuga/

LOUISIANA
Cane River Creole National
Historical Park
4386 Highway 494
Natchez, LA 71456
318-352-0383 phone
www.nps.gov/cari/

Jean Lafitte National
Historical Park
365 Canal Street, Suite 2400
New Orleans, LA 70130-2341
504-589-3882
www.nps.gov/jela/

Poverty Point State
Commemorative Area
PO Box 248
Epps, LA 71237
318-926-5492
www.nps.gov/popo/

MAINE
Acadia National Park & Saint
Croix Island International
Historical Site
PO Box 177
Bar Harbor, ME 04609-0177
207-288-3338
www.nps.gov/acad/home.htm

Penobscot Marine Museum
Exhibit: "An Ocean Going
Community: Searsport at Sea and
Ashore" and "Folklife in Penobscot
Bay, Maine"
5 Church Street
Searsport, ME 04974
207-548-2529
www.acadia.net/pmmuseum/

MARYLAND
Antietam National Battlefield
PO Box 158
Sharpsburg, MD 21782-0158
301-432-5124
www.nps.gov/anti/home.htm

Baltimore Museum of Industry
Exhibit: "The Industrial History of
Baltimore"
1415 Key Highway
Baltimore, MD 21230
410-727-4808
www.charm.net/~bmi

Chesapeake & Ohio Canal
National Historical Park
PO Box 4
Sharpsburg, MD 21782-0004
301-739-4200
www.nps.gov/choh/

Hampton National Historic Site
535 Hampton Lane
Towson, Maryland 21286-1397
410-823-1309
www.nps.gov/hamp/

Monocacy National Battlefield
4801 Urbana Pike
Frederick, MD 21703-7307
301-662-3515
www.nps.gov/mono/home.htm

Thomas Stone National
Historic Site
6655 Rose Hill Road
Port Tobacco, MD 20677
301-934-6027
www.nps.gov/thst/

MASSACHUSETTS

Adams National Historical Park
135 Adams Street
Quincy, MA 02169
617-773-1177
www.nps.gov/adam

Boston African American National
Historical Site
14 Beacon Street Suite 503
Boston, MA 02108-3704
617-742-5415
www.nps/gov/boaf

Boston National Historical Park
Charlestown Navy Yard
Building 107
Boston, MA 02129
617-242-5642
www.nps.gov/bost/home.htm

Concord Museum
Exhibit: "'Why Concord?' The
History of Concord,
Massachusetts"
200 Lexington Road
Concord, MA 01742
978-369-9763
www.concordmuseum.org

John F. Kennedy National
Historic Site
83 Beals Street
Brookline, MA 02446
617-566-7937
www.nps.gov/jofi/

Lowell National Historical Park
67 Kirk Street
Lowell, MA 01852-1029
978-970-5000
www.nps.gov/lowe

Minute Man National
Historical Park
174 Liberty Street
Concord, MA 01742-1705
978-369-6993
www.nps.gov/mima

National Yiddish Book Center
Exhibit: "A Portable Homeland"
1021 West Street
Amherst, MA 01002-3375
413-256-4900
www.yiddishbookcenter.org

Plimoth Plantation, Inc.
Exhibit: "Irreconcilable
Differences: 1620-92"
137 Warren Avenue
Plymouth, MA 02362
508-746-1622
www.plimoth.org

Salem Maritime National
Historical Site
174 Derby Street
Salem, MA 01970
978-740-1650
www.nps.gov/sama/more.htm

Saugus Iron Works National
Historical Site
244 Central Street
Saugus, MA 01906-2107
781-233-0050
www.nps.gov/sair

Springfield Armory National
Historical Site
One Armory Square
Springfield, MA 01105-1299
413-734-8551 x236
www.nps.gov/spar

MICHIGAN

Father Marquette National
Monument
720 Church Street
St. Ignace, MI 49781
906-643-9394
www.nps.gov

Henry Ford Museum &
Greenfield Village
Exhibit: "Made in America: The
History of the American Industrial
System"
20900 Oakwood Blvd
Dearborn, MI 48121
313-271-1620
www.hfmgv.org

Public Museum of Grand Rapids
Exhibits: "The Furniture City" and
"Anishinabek: The People of this
Place"
272 Pearl Street NW
Grand Rapids, MI 49505
616-456-3977
www.grmuseum.org

MINNESOTA

Grand Portage National
Monument
PO Box 668
Grand Marais, MN 55604-0668
218-387-2788
www.nps.gov/grpo/

Minnesota Historical Society
Exhibits: "Families," "Learn About
Our Past: The Story of the Mille
Lacs Band of Ojibwe," and
"Manoominikewin: Stories of
Wild Ricing in Minnesota"
345 Kellogg Blvd. West
St. Paul, MN 55102
615-296-6126/800-657-3773
www.mnhs.org

Pipestone National Monument
36 Reservation Avenue
Pipestone, MN 56164-1269
507-825-5464
www.nps.gov/pipe/welcome.htm

MISSISSIPPI

Natchez National Historical Park
640 South Canal Street
PO Box 1208
Natchez, MS 39121
601-442-7047
www.nps.gov/natc/

Old Capitol Museum of
Mississippi History
Exhibit: "Mississippi 1500-1800"
North State & Capitol Streets.
Jackson, MS 39205
601-359-6920
www.mdah.state.ms.us

Smith Robertson Museum &
Cultural Center
Exhibit: "From Field to Factory:
Afro-American Migration, 1915-40"
528 Bloom Street
Jackson, MS 39202
601-960-1457

Vicksburg National Military Park
3201 Clay Street
Vicksburg, MS 39183
601-636-0583
www.nps.gov/vick/home.htm

MISSOURI

George Washington Carver
National Monument
5646 Carver Road
Diamond, MO 64840-8314
417-325-4151
www.nps.gov/gwca/

Harry S Truman National
Historic Site
223 North Main Street
Independence, MO 64050
816-254-7199
www.nps.gov/hstr/

Missouri Historical Society
Exhibits: "St. Louis in the Gilded
Age" and "Meet Me at the Fair:
Memory, History, and the 1904
World's Fair"
Lindell & De Baliviere
St. Louis, MO 63112-0040
314-746-4599
www.mohistory.org

Ulysses S. Grant National
Historic Site
7400 Grant Road
St. Louis, MO 63123-1801
314-842-3298
www.nps.gov/ulsg/

MONTANA

Big Hole National Battlefield
PO Box 237
Wisdom, MT 59761-0237
406-689-3155
www.nps.gov/biho/

Grant-Kohrs Ranch
National Historical Site
PO Box 790
Deer Lodge, MT 59722-0790
406-846-2070
www.nps.gov/grko

Little Bighorn Battlefield National
Monument
PO Box 39
Crow Agency, MT 59022
406-638-2621
www.nps.gov/libi/

Western Heritage Center
Exhibit: "Our Place in the West:
The History of the Yellowstone
Valley, 1880-1940"
2822 Montana Avenue
Billings, MT 59101
406-256-6809, x21
www.ywhc.org

NEBRASKA
Agate Fossil Beds National
Monument
301 River Road
Harrison, NE 69346-2734
308-668-2211
www.nps.gov/agfo

Homestead National Monument
of America
Route 3
PO Box 47
Beatrice, NE 68310-9416
402-223-3514
www.nps.gov/home

Scotts Bluff National Monument
PO Box 27
190276 Highway 92W
Gering, NE 69341-0027
308-436-4340
www.nps.gov/scbl/

NEVADA
Death Valley National Park
PO Box 579
Death Valley, CA 92328
760-786-2331
www.nps.gov/deva/

NEW HAMPSHIRE
Strawbery Banke Museum
Exhibits: "Becoming Americans:
The Shapiro Story, 1898-1928"
and "Crossroads of Neighborhood
in Change: The Corner Grocery
Store at Strawbery Banke During
WWII"
454 Court Street
Portsmouth, NH 03802-0300
603-433-1100
www.strawberybanke.org/

New Hampshire Historical
Society
Exhibit: "New Hampshire
Through Many Eyes"
30 Park Street
Concord, NH 03301
603-225-3381
www.nhhistory.org

Saint-Gaudens National
Historic Site
RR 3, Box 73
Cornish, NH 03745
603-675-2175
www.nps.gov/saga/

NEW JERSEY
Edison National Historical Site
Main Street and Lakeside Avenue
West Orange, NJ 07052-5515
973-736-0550
www.nps.gov/edis

Morristown National
Historical Park
30 Washington Place
Morristown, NJ 07960-4299
973-539-2016
www.nps.gov/morr/

NEW MEXICO
Aztec Ruins National Monument
PO Box 640
Aztec, NM 87410-0640
505-334-6174 x31
www.nps.gov/azru/

Bandelier National Monument
HCR 1
PO Box 1 #15
Los Alamos, NM 87544
505-672-3861
www.nps.gov/band/

Chaco Culture National
Historical Park
PO Box 220
Nageezi, NM 87037-0220
505-786-7014
www.nps.gov/chcu/

El Malpais National Monument
PO Box 939
201 East Roosevelt Avenue
Grants, NM 87020-0939
505-285-4641
www.nps.gov/elma/

El Morro National Monument
Route 2
PO Box 43
Ramah, NM 87321
505-783-4226
www.nps.gov/elmo/

Maxwell Museum of
Anthropology
Exhibits: "People of the
Southwest" and "Ancestors"
University and Ash, NE
Albuquerque, NM 87131-1201
505-277-4405
www.unm.edu/~maxwell

Museum of Indian Arts & Culture
Exhibit: "Here, Now, and Always:
A Permanent Exhibition of
Southwestern Indian Culture
and Art"
Museum Plaza, Camino Lejo
Santa Fe, NM 87504
505-827-6344
www.miaclab.org/miac_frame.htm

Palace of the Governors
Exhibits: "Society Defined: The
Hispanic Resident of New
Mexico" and "Another Mexico:
Spanish Life on the Upper Rio
Grande"
105 West Palace Ave.
Santa Fe, NM 87504-2087
505-476-5100
www.nmculture.org/cgi-
bin/showInst.pl?InstID=POG

Petroglyph National Monument
6001 Unser Boulevard, NW
Albuquerque, NM 87120-2069
505-899-0205
www.nps.gov/petr/

Salinas Pueblo Missions National
Monument
PO Box 517
Mountainair, NM 87036
505-847-2585
www.nps.gov/sapu/

NEW YORK
Adirondack Museum
Exhibit: "A Peopled Wilderness"
Rt. 28 North & Rt. 30
Blue Mountain Lake, NY 12812-
0099
518-352-7311, x101
www.adkmuseum.org

Brooklyn Historical Society
Exhibit: "BROOKLYNWORKS:
150 Years of Work in an American
City" (scheduled to open June 2000)
128 Pierrepont Street
Brooklyn, NY 11201
718-254-9830
www.brooklynhistory.org

Eleanor Roosevelt National
Historic Site
519 Albany Post Road
Hyde Park, NY 12538
914-229-9115
www.nps.gov/elro/

Federal Hall
26 Wall Street
New York, NY 10005
212-825-6888
www.nps.gov/feha/

Fort Stanwix National Monument
112 East Park Street
Rome, NY 13440
315-336-2090
www.nps.gov/fost/

Home of Franklin D. Roosevelt
National Historic Site
519 Albany Post Road
Hyde Park, NY 12538
914-229-9115
www.nps.gov/hofr/

Lower East Side Tenement
Museum
Exhibit: "1863 Tenement House
Tour"
97 Orchard Street
New York, NY 10002
212-431-0233
www.wnet.org/tenement

Martin Van Buren National
Historic Site
1013 Old Post Road
Kinderhook, NY 12106
518-758-9689
www.nps.gov/mava/

Museum of Chinese
in the Americas
Exhibit: "Where is Home?:
Chinese in the Americas"
70 Mulberry St., 2nd floor
New York, NY 10013
212-619-4785

New York Botanical Garden
Exhibit: "Nature and Culture in
the Garden"
200th Street & Southern Blvd.
The Bronx, NY 10458
718-817-8700
www.nybg.org

Sagamore Hill National
Historical Site
20 Sagamore Hill Road
Oyster Bay, NY 11771
516-922-4788
www.nps.gov/sahi/

Saint Marie de Gannentaha
Historical Site
Onondaga Lane Park
Liverpool, NY 13088
315-492-6576
www.tier.net/isa/stemarie.htm

Saint Paul's Church National
Historic Site
897 South Columbus Avenue
Mount Vernon, NY
914-667-4116
www.nps.gov/sapa/

Saratoga National Historical Park
648 Route 32
Stillwater, NY 12170-1604
518-664-9821 x224
www.nps.gov/sara/

South Street Seaport Museum
Exhibit: "World Port, New York"
(scheduled to open 2000)
207 Front Street
New York, NY 10038
212-748-8725
www.southstseaport.org

Vanderbilt Mansion National
Historic Site
519 Albany Post Road
Hyde Park, NY 12538
914-229-9115
www.nps.gov/vama/

Women's Rights National
Historical Park
136 Fall Street
Seneca Falls, NY 13148
315-568-2991
www.nps.gov/wori

NORTH CAROLINA
Carl Sandburg Home National
Historic Site
1928 Little River Road
Flat Rock, NC 28731
828-693-4178
www.nps.gov/carl/

Fort Raleigh National
Historical Site
Route 1, PO Box 675
Manteo, NC 27954-9708
252-473-5772
www.nps.gov/fora/raleigh.htm

Moores Creek National Battlefield
40 Patriots Hall Drive
Currie, NC 28435-0069
910-283-5591
www.nps.gov/mocr/

Wright Brothers National
Historic Site
PO Box 2539
Kill Devil Hills, NC 27948
252-441-7430
www.nps.gov/wrbr/

NORTH DAKOTA
Fort Union Trading Post National
Historic Site
15550 Hwy. 1804
Williston, ND 58801
701-572-9083
www.nps.gov/fous/

Knife River Indian Villages
National Historic Site
PO Box 9
Stanton, ND 58571-0009
701-745-3309
www.nps.gov/knri/

NORTHERN MARIANAS
American Memorial Park
National Park Service
PO Box 5198-CHRB
Saipan, MP 96950-5198
670-234-7207
www.nps.gov/amme/

OHIO
Dayton Aviation Heritage
National Historical Park
PO Box 9280
Wright Brothers Station
Dayton, OH 45409-9280
937-225-7705
www.nps.gov/daav/

Hopewell Culture National
Historical Park
16062 State Route 104
Chillicothe, OH 45601-8694
740-774-1125
www.nps.gov/hocu

James A. Garfield National
Historical Site
8095 Mentor Avenue
Mentor, OH 44060-5753
440-255-8722
www.nps.gov/jaga/

William Howard Taft National
Historical Site
2038 Auburn Avenue
Cincinnati, OH 45219-3025
513-684-3262
www.nps.gov/wiho/

OKLAHOMA
Washita Battlefield National
Historic Site
PO Box 890
Cheyenne, Oklahoma 73628
580-497-2742
www.nps.gov/waba/

OREGON
Fort Clatsop National Monument
92343 Fort Clatsop Road
Astoria, OR 97103-9197
503-861-2471
www.nps.gov/focl/home.htm

High Desert Museum
Exhibit: "By Hand Through
Memory"
59800 South Highway 97
Bend, OR 97702-7963
541-382-4754
www.highdesert.org

McLoughlin House National
Historical Site
713 Center
Oregon City, OR 97045
503-656-5146
www.mcloughlinhouse.org

PENNSYLVANIA
Allegheny Portage Railroad
National Historical Site
110 Federal Park Road
Gallitzin, PA 16641
814-886-6100
www.nps.gov/alpo

Carnegie Museum of
Natural History
Alcoa Foundation Hall of
American Indians
4400 Forbes Avenue
Pittsburgh, PA 15213
412-622-3131
www.clpgh.org

Eisenhower National
Historical Site
97 Taneytown Road
Gettysburg, PA 17325-2804
717-338-9114
www.nps.gov/eise

Fort Necessity National Battlefield
One Washington Parkway
Farmington, PA 15437-9514
724-329-5512
www.nps.gov/fone

Friendship Hill National
Historical Site
One Washington Parkway
Farmington, PA 15437
724-725-9190
www.nps.gov/frhi

Gettysburg National Military Park
PO Box 1080
Gettysburg, PA 17325-2998
717-334-1124
www.nps.gov/gett

Gloria Dei Church National
Historical Site
Delaware Avenue and
Christian Street
Philadelphia, PA 19106
215-389-1513
www.nps.gov/glde/

Hopewell Furnace National
Historical Site
Two Mark Bird Lane
Elverson, PA 19520-9505
610-582-8773
www.nps.gov/hofu/index.html

Independence National
Historical Park
313 Walnut Street
Philadelphia, PA 19106-2778
215-597-8974
www.nps.gov/inde

Independence Seaport Museum
Exhibit: "Home Port Philadelphia"
Penn's Landing Waterfront
211 South Columbus Blvd &
Walnut Street
Philadelphia, PA 19106
215-925-5439
www.libertynet.org/~seaport

Johnstown Flood National
Memorial
c/o Allegheny Portage Railroad
National Historical Site
110 Federal Pack Road
Gallitzin, PA 16641
814-886-6100
www.nps.gov/jofl

Morris Arboretum,
University of Pennsylvania
Exhibit: "Healing Plants:
Medicines Across Time and
Cultures"
100 Northwestern Avenue
Philadelphia, PA 19118
215-247-5777
www.upenn.edu/morris

Senator John Heinz Pittsburgh
Regional History Center
Exhibit: "Points in Time: Building
a Life in Western Pennsylvania,
1750-Today"
1212 Smallman Street
Pittsburgh, PA 15222
412-454-6000
www.pghhistory/org

Steamtown National Historic Site
150 South Washington Avenue
Scranton, PA 18503
570-340-5200
www.nps.gov/stea/

University of Pennsylvania
Museum of Archaeology and
Anthropology
Exhibit: "Living in Balance: The
Universe of the Hopi, Zuni,
Navajo, and Apache"
33rd & Spruce Streets
Philadelphia, PA 19104
215-898-4001
www.Upenn.edu/museum/

PUERTO RICO
San Juan National Historic Site
Fort San Cristobal
Norzagaray Street
San Juan, PR 00901
787-729-6777
www.nps.gov/saju/

RHODE ISLAND
Museum of Newport History
Exhibit: "Hope and Speculation:
The Landscape of Newport
History"
82 Touro Street
Newport, RI 02840
401-846-0813
www.newporthistorical.com

Museum of Work & Culture
Exhibit: "La Survivance: An
Exhibition About French
Canadians in Woonsocket"
110 Benevolent Street
Providence, RI 02906
401-331-8575
www.rihs.org (under construction)

Roger Williams National
Memorial
282 North Main Street
Providence, RI 02903
401-521-7266
www.nps.gov/rowi/

Touro Synagogue National
Historic Site
85 Touro Street
Newport, RI 02840
401-847-4794
www.nps.gov/tosy/

SOUTH CAROLINA
Charles Pinckney National
Historic Site
1214 Middle Street
Sullivan's Island, SC 29462-9748
843-881-5516
www.nps.gov/chpi/

Fort Moultrie
1214 Middle St.
Sullivan's Island, SC 29482
843-883-3123
www.nps.gov/fomo/

Fort Sumter National Monument
1214 Middle Street
Sullivans Island, SC 29482
843-883-3123
www.nps.gov/fosu/fosu.htm

Historic Camden Revolutionary
War Site
222 Broad Street
Camden, SC 29020
803-432-9841
www.nsp.gov

Kings Mountain National
Military Park
2625 Park Road
Blacksburg, SC 29702
864-936-7921
www.nps.gov/kimo/

SOUTH DAKOTA
Jewel Cave National Monument
RR1 Box 60 AA
Custer, SD 57730
605-673-2288
www.nps.gov/jeca/

Mount Rushmore National
Memorial
PO Box 268
Keystone, SD 57751
605-574-2523
www.nps.gov/moru/

South Dakota State Historical
Society, Cultural Heritage
Exhibit: "Proving Up"
900 Governors Drive
Pierre, SD 57501-2217
605-773-3458
www.state.sd.us/state/executive/
deca/cultural/museum.htm

TENNESSEE
Andrew Johnson National
Historical Site
PO Box 1088
Greenville, TN 37744
423-638-3551
www.nps.gov/anjo/index.htm

Fort Donelson National Battlefield
PO Box 434
Dover, TN 37058-0434
931-232-5348
www.nps.gov/fodo/

Shiloh National Military Park
1055 Pittsburg Landing Road
Shiloh, TN 38376
901-689-5275
www.nps.gov/shil/

Stones River National Battlefield
3501 Old Nashville Highway
Murfreesboro, TN 37129
615-893-9501
www.nps.gov/stri/

TEXAS
Chamizal National Monument
800 South San Marcial
El Paso, TX 79905
915-532-7273
www.nps.gov/cham/

Fort Davis National Historical Site
PO Box 1456
Fort Davis, TX 79734
915-426-3224
www.nps.gov/foda/

Lyndon B. Johnson National
Historical Park
PO Box 329
Johnson City, TX 78636
830-868-7128
www.nps.gov/lyjo/

Palo Alto Battlefield National
Historical Site
1623 Central Boulevard
Room 213
Brownsville, TX 78520-8326
956-541-2785
www.nps.gov/paal/

San Antonio Missions National
Historical Park
2202 Roosevelt Avenue
San Antonio, TX 78210
210-534-8833
www.nps.gov/saan/

UTAH
Golden Spike National
Historical Site
PO Box 897
Brigham City, UT 84302-0897
435-471-2209 x21
www.nps.gov/gosp/

VERMONT
Marsh-Billings-Rockefeller
National Historical Park
PO Box 178
54 Elm Street
Woodstock, VT 05091
802-457-3368
www.nps.gov/mabi/

VIRGIN ISLANDS
Buck Island Reef National
Monument
Danish Custom House,
Kings Wharf
2100 Church Street #100
Christiansted, VI 00820-4611
340-773-1460
www.nps.gov/buis/

Christiansted National
Historic Site
PO Box 160
Christiansted, VI 00821
340-773-1460
www.nps.gov/chri/

VIRGINIA
Appomattox Court House
National Historical Park
PO Box 218
Appomattox, VA 24522
804-352-8987
www.nps.gov/apco

Arlington House
The Robert E. Lee Memorial
c/o National Park Service
George Washington Memorial
Parkway
Turkey Run Park
McLean, VA 22101
Telephone: 703-557-0613
www.nps.gov/arho/

Booker T. Washington National
Monument
12130 BTW Highway
Hardy, VA 24101-3968
540-721-2094
www.nps.gov/bowa

Colonial National Historical Park
PO Box 210
Yorktown, VA 23690
757-898-3400
www.nps.gov/colo/

George Washington Birthplace
National Monument
1732 Popes Creek Road
Washington's Birthplace, VA 22443
804-224-1732
www.nps.gov/gewa/splitpage.htm

Maggie L Walker National
Historic Site
c/o Richmond National
Battlefield Park
3215 East Broad Street
Richmond, VA 23223
804-771-2017
www.nps.gov/malw

Manassas National Battlefield Park
12521 Lee Highway
Manassas, VA 20109-2005
703-361-1339
www.nps.gov/mana/home.htm

Museum of the Confederacy
Exhibit: "Before Freedom Came:
African American Life in the
Antebellum South"
1201 East Clay Street
Richmond, VA 23219
804-649-1861
www.moc.org

Petersburg National Battlefield
1539 Hickory Hill Road
Petersburg, VA 23803
804-732-3531
www.nps.gov/pete/pe_info.htm

Richmond National Battlefield
3215 Broad Street
Richmond, VA 23223
804-226-1981
www.nps.gov/rich/home.htm

WASHINGTON
Burke Museum of Natural History
and Culture
Exhibit: "Pacific Voices"
University of Washington Campus
Seattle, WA 98195
206-543 7907
www.washington.edu/
burkemuseum/index.html

Fort Vancouver National
Historical Site
612 East Reserve Street
Vancouver, WA 98661-3811
360-696-7655
www.nps.gov/fova/

Klondike Gold Rush National
Historical Park
117 South Main Street
Seattle, WA 98104-2540
206-553-7220
www.nps.gov/klgo

San Juan Island National
Historical Park
PO Box 429
Friday Harbor, WA 98250
360-378-2902
www.nps.gov/sajh/home.htm

Whitman Mission National
Historic Site
Route 2, PO Box 247
Walla Walla, WA 99362-9699
509-522-6360
www.nps.gov/whmi

WEST VIRGINIA
Harpers Ferry National
Historical Park
PO Box 65
Harpers Ferry, WV 25425
304-535-6298
www.nps.gov/hafe/home.htm

WISCONSIN
Milwaukee Public Museum
Exhibit: "A Tribute to Survival"
800 West Wells Street
Milwaukee, WI 53233
414-278-2700
www.mpm.edu

Chippewa Valley Museum
"Settlement and Survival: Building
Towns in the Chippewa Valley,
1850-1925"
1204 Carson Park Drive
Eau Claire, WI 54702
715-834-7871
www.cvmusuem.com

WYOMING
Buffalo Bill Historical Center
Exhibit: "Plains Indian Museum"
720 Sheridan Ave.
Cody, WY 82414
307-587-4771, x 0
www.truewest.com/BBHC/

Fort Laramie National
Historical Site
HC 72
PO Box 389
Fort Laramie, WY 82212-9501
307-837-2221
www.nps.gov

The National Endowment for the Humanities wants to thank our outside consultants:

Peggy Barber, American Library Association
Bernard Bailyn, Harvard University
Peggy Bulger, American Folklife Center, Library of Congress
Evelyn Figueroa, Smithsonian Institution
Barbara Franco, Historical Society of Washington, DC
Rhonda Frevert, The Newberry Library
Ellen Gehres, Denver Public Library
James Horton, George Washington University
Alan Kraut, American University
Richard Kurin, Center for Folklife Programs and Cultural Studies, Smithsonian Institution
Timothy Meagher, The Catholic University
Page Putnam Miller, National Coordinating Committee for the Promotion of History
Steven Newsome, Anacostia Museum, Smithsonian Institution
Judith Prowse Reid, Local History and Genealogy Reading Room, Library of Congress
David Rencher, Family History Department, Church of Jesus Christ of Latter-day Saints
Roy Rosenzweig, Center for Media and History, George Mason University
Dorothy Schwartz, Maine Humanities Council
Re-Cheng Tsang, California Council for the Humanities
Marie Tyler-McGraw, National Park Service

Contributors:
Fun for the Family—Mira Bartók
Saving Your Family's Treasures—Jane Long

Credits

MY HISTORY IS AMERICA'S HISTORY ★

Project Director:	Patti Van Tuyl
Design:	Watermark Design Office
Writing:	Robert D. Selim
Historical Research:	Mary Beth Corrigan
Picture Research:	Bonnie Fitzgerald
Coordination:	Hank Grasso

Cover background: Photo courtesy Smithsonian Institution, National Museum of American History, other photographs and memorabilia from private collections, "The Welch Brothers," West Virginia Division of Culture and History Page 8: Beinecke Rare Book & Manuscript Library, Yale University Page 9: Upper right photograph Ewing Galloway, center photographs courtesy Velma Skidmore, bottom center photograph Beinecke Rare Book & Manuscript Library, Yale University Page 10: Upper left photograph courtesy Jerry Curley, center photograph "Roxanne and Rena Swentzel" by Annie Sahlin, lower right photograph by T.K. Ransom Page 11: Photographs courtesy Jerry Curley Page 12: Photograph by William R. Ferris Page 13: Photograph by William R. Ferris Page 14: Upper left private collection, lower courtesy Velma Skidmore Page 15: Private collection Page 16: Photographs courtesy Angela Walton-Raji Page 17: Upper and lower right photographs courtesy Oklahoma Historical Society, center right courtesy Angela Walton-Raji Page 18: Upper left courtesy Angela Walton-Raji, center photograph courtesy Oklahoma Historical Society Page 19: Upper right courtesy Angela Walton-Raji, center photograph courtesy Oklahoma Historical Society Page 20: Memorabilia from private collections Page 21: Photographs courtesy Marie Locke and Nancy Montgomery Page 22: Photographs courtesy Marie Locke and Nancy Montgomery Page 23: Photographs courtesy Marie Locke and Nancy Montgomery Page 24: Upper left, lower left, center bottom, center spread photographs Ewing Galloway, upper center private collection Page 25: Center spread, lower right photographs Ewing Galloway, upper right private collection Page 26: Photographs courtesy Julia Fong Page 28: Upper left courtesy Tom Madrid, lower left and lower center photographs courtesy Museum of New Mexico Page 29: Photographs courtesy Tom Madrid Page 30: Ewing Galloway Page 31: Maine Humanities Council Page 32: Upper left courtesy Angela Peterson, lower left private collection Page 33: Center photograph courtesy State Historical Society of Wisconsin, upper and lower right courtesy Angela Peterson Page 34: Upper left, upper center, lower center courtesy State Historical Society of Wisconsin, center photo private collection Page 35: Center illustration National Park Service, artist John Dawson, left center, upper right, and lower right courtesy Angela Peterson Page 36: Photograph courtesy Angela Walton-Raji Page 37: Comstock, Inc. Page 38: Comstock, Inc. Page 39: Upper right photograph Comstock, Inc., lower photographs private collection Page 40: Photograph courtesy Sal Romano Page 41: Photographs courtesy Sal Romano Page 42: Upper left photograph courtesy Maine Humanities Council, center left photograph private collection, center photograph "Roxanne and Rena Swentzel" by Annie Sahlin Page 43: Upper right, center, and lower center photographs courtesy Maine Humanities Council, right center photograph "In Search of Common Ground: Senior Citizens and Community Life at Potomac Gardens," Anacostia Museum Page 44: Upper left photograph courtesy Orcas Island Historical Museum, lower left and lower right photographs courtesy Maine Humanities Council Page 45: Upper right, center, and lower right photographs courtesy Orcas Island Historical Museum, lower left photograph by T.K. Ransom Page 46: Upper left, lower left, and lower center photographs private collections, center left illustration "Louisiana Indians of the Bayou" by Alfred Boisseau courtesy New Orleans Museum of Art, middle left lower photograph courtesy Smithsonian Institution, lower right photograph courtesy Maine Humanities Council Page 47: Upper right photograph private collection, center right photograph Library of Congress, lower photographs courtesy Maine Humanities Council Page 48: Upper left photograph courtesy Maine Humanities Council, lower left courtesy Southern Media Archive, Center for the Study of Southern Culture, University of Mississippi, center photograph © Chinese Historical Society of America #CHSA04291 Daniel K.E. Ching Collection, lower center private collection, lower right courtesy Indiana Historical Society #79072E Page 49: Upper right, center right courtesy Julia Fong, lower left illustration © Chinese Historical Society of America #CHSA04485 Daniel K.E. Ching Collection Page 50: Upper left © Chinese Historical Society of America #CHSA04291 Daniel K.E. Ching Collection, left center Ewing Galloway, center photographs courtesy Julia Fong Page 51: Upper right photograph courtesy California State Library, center photograph © Chinese Historical Society of America #CHSA04459C Daniel K.E. Ching Collection, lower center private collection Page 52: Photographs courtesy Julia Fong Page 53: Left photograph courtesy Sandy Spring Museum, left center photograph Library of Congress, center courtesy New York Yankees, center right photograph The Catholic University of America, right photograph courtesy Smithsonian Institution, National Museum of American History Page 54: Private collections Page 55: Upper right photo courtesy Smithsonian Institution, lower right private collections Page 56: Private collections Page 57: Upper right, center, and lower photographs private collections, right lower center photograph courtesy Smithsonian Institution Page 58: Upper left, lower left, and center photographs private collections, lower center photograph courtesy Smithsonian Institution, National Museum of American History Page 59: Upper right, lower photographs private collections, center left illustration courtesy The Catholic University of America Page 60: Upper and lower left photographs courtesy Smithsonian Institution, lower right private collection Page 61: Private collections Page 62: Upper left, lower photographs private collections, center left photograph Library of Congress Page 63: Private collections Page 64: Private collections Page 65: Private collections Page 66: Private collections Page 67: Upper left, lower right private collections, lower right courtesy Smithsonian Institution Page 68: Photograph by William R. Ferris Page 69: Photograph by William R. Ferris Page 71: Private collection Page 73: Private collection Page 75: The Cleveland Plain Dealer Page 77: Library of Congress Page 79: Library of Congress Page 81: Private collection Page 83: Photograph by William R. Ferris Page 85: Photograph by William R. Ferris Page 87: Photograph by William R. Ferris Page 89: Private collection Page 91: Photograph courtesy Jerry Curley Page 93: Photograph by William R. Ferris Page 95: Private collection Page 97: Private collection

My History Is America's History
Contributing Partners

National Endowment for the Humanities

Created in 1965 as an independent federal agency, NEH supports learning in history, literature, philosophy, and other areas of the humanities. NEH grants enrich classroom learning, create and preserve knowledge through research and preservation, and bring ideas to life through public television, radio, and new technologies, museum exhibitions, and programs in libraries and other community places. Honoring its commitment to make excellence in the humanities a part of every American's life, NEH has worked closely with its generous contributing and supporting partners to develop *My History Is America's History.*

White House Millennium Council

The White House Millennium Council was created by the President and Mrs. Clinton to lead the country in a celebration of the new millennium by initiating and recognizing national and local projects that "Honor the Past — Imagine the Future." The Council encourages communities, organizations, and individuals to support and participate in historical projects that contribute in educational, creative, and productive ways to America's commemoration of this milestone. *My History Is America's History* is designated as an official project of the White House Millennium Council.

President's Committee on the Arts and the Humanities

The President's Committee on the Arts and the Humanities encourages private sector support and public appreciation of the value of the arts and the humanities, through projects, publications, and meetings. Appointed by the President, the Committee comprises leading citizens from the private sector who have an interest in and commitment to the humanities and the arts. The Committee is providing leadership support for *My History Is America's History*.

 ### genealogy.com

Genealogy.com

Genealogy.com is a pioneering developer of several computer-based genealogy tools including software programs and online resources. These tools enable users to go online to learn about genealogy, to conduct their genealogy research through proprietary search engines and databases, and to build and publish their family trees. Genealogy.com programs and web sites have received numerous awards and honors for excellence, innovation, and ease of use. Genealogy.com has contributed its expertise and financial support in developing the **www.myhistory.org** website.

PSINet Inc.

PSINet is a global facilities-based Internet Protocol (IP) data communications carrier focused on the business marketplace. One of the world's first and largest independent commercial Internet service providers, PSINet offers a broad set of high-speed corporate LAN connectivity services that support managed security and guaranteed Internet, Intranet, electronic commerce, Web hosting services, and services for other carriers and ISPs. Managed hosting services for **www.myhistory.org** are being contributed by PSINet Inc.

National Association of Broadcasters

The National Association of Broadcasters (NAB), a nonprofit membership organization, represents the radio and television industry, providing leadership and resources to nearly 6,000 member radio and television stations and to broadcasters at-large, and through its ongoing support of public service campaigns for the American people. NAB is helping to provide information to the public about *My History Is America's History* through its member television and radio stations, which reach millions of people across the nation.

Heritage Preservation

Heritage Preservation

Heritage Preservation is a national nonprofit advocate and resource for the proper care of works of art, books and archives, documents and photographs, architecture and monuments, natural science specimens, and family heirlooms. Heritage Preservation has worked closely with the National Endowment for the Humanities to develop "Saving Your Family Treasures," the preservation component of *My History Is America's History*.

FamilyFun

FamilyFun

FamilyFun, a magazine for parents with young children, is an information sourcebook for activities that families can do together. *FamilyFun* is published by Buena Vista Magazines, Inc., a division of The Walt Disney Company. The activities for families featured in *My History Is America's History* have been contributed by *FamilyFun.*

 HOUGHTON MIFFLIN

Houghton Mifflin Company

Houghton Mifflin is a leading publisher of textbooks, instructional technology, assessments, and other educational materials for the elementary and secondary school and college markets. The Company also publishes an extensive line of reference works, fiction and non-fiction for adults and young readers, and multimedia entertainment products. Houghton Mifflin Company has contributed historical reference information for the **www.myhistory.org** website.